The Casual Millionaire

The Casual Millionaire:
Wealth by Intention

Tonja Demoff

Arbor Books
2007

The Casual Millionaire
Copyright © 2007 Tonja Demoff
Published by Arbor Books

For more information about this title, please contact:

Arbor Books
244 Madison Ave, #254
New York, NY 10016
877-822-2500

Book design by Arbor Books
www.arborbooks.com

Printed in the United States

The Casual Millionaire
Tonja Demoff

1. Title 2. Author 3. Non-fiction, life-enhancement, real estate, wealth building, motivation
Business/Real Estate/Success

Library of Congress Control Number: 2006905050

ISBN: 0-9777764-9-2

Acknowledgements

I want to thank Spirit for blessing my life with the ultimate experience of loving and of being loved. I am surrounded by business partners who clearly support and embody my vision by making it a vision that they too share.

A special thank you to the partners at the Tonja Demoff Companies, who make each and every day one to remember and cherish. Thank you for being such a loving group. Thank you for being soooooo much fun!

Thank you is in order for a few special people who touch my life daily:

Marianne Williamson, for being so clearly genuine. You have been a wonderful example.

Kathe Morgan, for your creativity, loving sarcasm and friendship—it's inspiring.

Kathy Brown, for sharing yourself, your irresistible charm and your quick-witted humor in such a supportive and empowering way.

Toby "Gibraltar," you are my rock, the foundation for which all of this is enjoyable. Thank you for all that you are and for all that you have helped me to see within myself. Your love moves the truth within me to fully express, and it is my love for you that allows me to shine, walking the walk of the casual millionaire.

Contents

The Casual
Millionaire

Introduction

If you are still not sure who you are, what you want in life and whom you wish to become, but know success is your destination, *The Casual Millionaire* is dedicated to you. It's about unraveling the confusion within, exploring your own truth, finding your happy zone and the hidden source of creativity, building your dream into reality and learning how to take from the universe the inspiration and encouragement you need to live your ideal life. It's also about achieving wholeness and developing a harmonious mind-set with which to create an inner balance that will encourage you to invest your time and energy in "aggressive growth investments," earning large dividends. Like in real estate, the focus is on location, timing and being knowledgeable enough to recognize and seize a potentially golden opportunity. In addition, knowing who you are and deciding on where and when you want to locate yourself is the key to achievement.

Since the concepts outlined in this book worked for me, I decided to share my experiences and the knowledge I accumulated to reach my desired destination, to hasten your journey towards achieving the personal and professional affluence you desire. One of the most important lessons I've learned on my "travels" is that it's not just about receiving; it's about giving, and giving back to the universe.

I was born in a small town in Indiana to parents who were not in a position to finance my higher education pursuits, and I was raised by my grandparents. Realistic about the family's economic challenges, my grandmother, whom I affectionately referred to as Mom, envisioned a military option as a means for me to delve further into my studies. One day, she escorted me to the recruitment center, looked me directly in the eyes and said, "Tonja, there are four branches—pick one! If you ask me, I would suggest the Air Force." Her words seemed wise. Convinced, I followed her advice, energized with the vibrancy of youthful expectations.

With my intention set on enlisting, earning a degree and then turning on my heels to march back into the civilian world, I started my military career in the Air Force at the Lackland Base in San Antonio, Texas, as a recruit in basic training.

I soon learned I was obliged to adhere to an impeccable appearance code. Shoes had to glisten while identity tags and ribbons had to be in precise alignment. There were no exceptions, no procrastinating and absolutely no compromising. It was not just a matter of wearing a clean, pressed uniform; it was an order for unassailable perfection. Later in my career, as a military trainer, I was expected to be above faultless. Accordingly, I changed my uniform twice a day, since I worked long hours and was required to be appropriately dressed from 4:15 a.m. until 10:00 p.m.!

Early on, I discovered a love for the Air Force, the interesting variety of people I met and the exciting opportunities life in the military offered. The training and discipline were invigorating and the travel was an enriching experience. Coming from a dysfunctional family, I learned early on the devastating pitfalls and consequences bred from an undisciplined and chaotic lifestyle. I found the radical, 180-degree swing towards structure and restraint that life in the military offered an appealing alternative. The rigorous training, meshed with a philosophy of constructive authority, proved to be valuable. I was motivated, gained self-confidence and was ready to begin my climb to the top.

I was sent to Lowry Air Force Base in Colorado to study Inventory Management and upon completion of the course, I was transferred to Malmstrom Air Force Base in Great Falls, Montana.

Although I had not been in the service for a lengthy period of time, and contrary to the opinions of those who believed that at just eighteen years of age I was not old enough, I applied for the military training instructor position. Firm in my intention and convinced of my potential to accomplish my goal, I planned my strategy. I began to phone the decision makers and persuaded them I was capable of handling the job and its serious responsibilities.

It worked! My words persuaded, I got the assignment and was sent to the Military Training Instructor School. Once again, the discipline was riveting. It sharpened my wits, revved me up and broadened my vision! I felt undefeatable! I completed the course. I was the youngest ranking person to earn a Blue Rope during my career, a prestigious honor awarded exclusively to the top 10 percent.

Merit badges and certificates of education testimonials

are energizing self-esteem boosters. However, you really do not know the value of what you've assimilated until you've applied it, simply because hoarding the knowledge you've accumulated is comparable to deleting it! If left immobile, it expires!

From the training instructor school, I learned a highly regimented teaching format. Later in life, this proved to be a phenomenal asset when I opted to finally put in action my long-term intentions to become involved in a real estate career.

Upon completion of the training program, I applied to the recruiter school, was accepted and transferred to Colorado Springs. After this tour, I returned to Lackland Air Force Base as the Military Training Instructor School instructor. My "job description" entailed teaching the basic training instructors how to fulfill their obligations as military training instructors. Suddenly, I noticed the discipline mystique I found so captivating was gone! Although I dressed in uniform, I was not assigned to a base and was no longer restricted in my actions.

I was responsible for thirty-six high schools and given an itinerary that involved traveling across Colorado and Kansas. The only expectations placed upon me were to reach a certain quota of recruits. Unsatisfied with the less than exhilarating assignment, I decided to set my own guidelines and goals. This step would motivate me and give me control over my own self-worth. It would allow me to continue maturing into who I wanted to be.

I noticed that when I addressed the students dressed in my Air Force uniform, they seemed intimated. Their rigid body language told me I was not breaking ground. They were reticent and totally disinterested in what I had to communicate. My severe appearance produced an almost instinctive reaction to pull away and as a result, the students closed themselves off. They saw in me an authority figure similar to their parents and automatically rejected what I had come to promote. In essence, they had constructed a separating wall, a fortress I was unable to penetrate.

However, neither enthusiastic nor accepting of my initial failings, I changed my strategy and appeared in civilian dress. It was like magic! The kids sprang forward, listened to what I had to say and took the initiative to engage me in conversation. I started to build relationships and began attending their sporting events wearing my Air Force t-shirt with a pair of jeans and tennis shoes. I was a magnet! The kids flocked around, asked questions and signed up!

I became the number one recruiter for four consecutive years. Yet, despite my extraordinary track record, the Air Force reprimanded me for working out of uniform. They had imposed certain conditions I felt impeded creativity and they had given me restrictive orders! After all, this was the military!

I defended my position, explained my strategy, demonstrated the exceptional results I had achieved as the number one recruiting agent and assured them I was not disrespecting the Air Force but building trust in these high schools' students who were showing more availability and interest since I dropped the uniform. However, my reasoning was adamantly rejected. In the words of William Shakespeare, "The cannons…spit forth their indignation!" Clearly, this was not the script the obstinate, inflexible and steadfast military wanted to see played out! In truth, this was a "reciprocity moment" because resolute in my thinking, I could not play by their rules!

Continuing to do it my way, I began to schedule seminars involving the entire junior and senior classes instead of strategizing to recruit on a one-to-one basis. The outcome was phenomenal. I enlisted kids in mass numbers, enrolling them in a delayed enlistment program. Instead of just waiting by the sidelines, I had them come to my office to work. I turned the "intermission" between graduating high school and being inducted in the military into a pre-orientation period, encouraging them to practice marching as an introduction to basic training! I believe guidance is a worthwhile prelude to instruction and experience and strongly felt it was a helping hand for the kids, making their transition from civilian to military status smoother.

I noticed that the more discipline I instilled in the kids, the more hyped up they became about actually beginning basic training. They loved my particular brand of discipline, which was different from the dry, parental designed, authority-restriction control type. Discipline should be productivity-friendly or its *raison d'etre* becomes non-existent. It should not throttle self-expression, disengage personality development or squash creativity. This type of discipline serves only to breed anxiety, frustration and unhappiness. Instead, I incorporated motivation, potential development and accomplishment as part of my discipline line of attack. The kids gained impetus, were inspired and driven. It was breathtaking! What seemed to be just a bit of minutia in a wide vision actually represented so much hope.

Although I loved dressing in uniform, I realized I had to sacrifice my personal preferences if I wanted to get the job done and give my best performance. In that moment, it was important to relate to my audience and adapt to the environment! It was a lucrative lesson I never forgot!

Ten years, ten months and ten days after enlisting in the Air Force, I left the military. I stepped "outside the box." I knew I wanted to go further. I felt it was time to continue remodeling my mind-set and add a few more parts to the person I hoped to become. Until then, I had excelled at training and selling! But despite my success, I was searching for an identity. I had to find out who I was going to be and what was going to do it for me! This marked a turning point in my life, and the beginning of my journey to becoming a casual woman.

Not long after, while sitting on the beach in Hawaii, reading a newspaper, I noticed an insert in the classifieds: public speaker wanted for Mutual of New York Life Insurance Company. I applied for the position in Honolulu, was hired on the spot and advised to get my insurance license. This was a very different vehicle from the military, but I was determined to race it to the finish line!

Once again, I wanted to do things my way. I didn't see the correlation between conducting seminars and getting an insurance license. I addressed the branch manager with my plan. I outlined my idea of holding seminars and inviting all the agents in the room to create excitement over the products being offered. He was open to my suggestion and invited me to present my idea at a company meeting attended by forty-two agents.

As a novice to the profession, I was not received enthusiastically. Defiant eyes met my gaze and I was "informed" I did not have enough experience to sell insurance and had to obtain my license before they would give me any credibility. Motivated by the new challenge, I set my mind on nullifying the validity of their consideration and inquired what exactly they expected of me to change their mistrust in my capabilities.

"Tonja," they said, "if you sell four insurance policies in one month, we'll take you seriously!" They knew this was a herculean task, first because I had recently re-located, didn't know anyone and was without contacts, and second because I was taking my first steps in the insurance world! The challenge was enticing and too exciting to refuse. I accepted, and I immediately enrolled in a course to obtain my insurance license. Then I decided what tactics I would use to accomplish my purpose.

A licensed insurance agent, I drove out to Hickam Air Force Base and contacted the people in separation, who were transitioning from the military to civilian life. Although they were unaware, once discharged, they would loose their Servicemen's Group Life Insurance Policy! I decided to give a seminar and present my offerings.

I dressed in a suit for my first speaking engagement before a group of military personnel who were in their battle dress uniforms, also known as BDUs! They were dressed down and I was overdressed and feeling not quite at ease. That day, I sold two policies. Unsatisfied with my productivity quotient, I realized I had to change my strategy if I wanted to increase my sales. I thought to myself, Ben Franklin was right: "Eat to please thyself, but dress to please others" was a good principle to follow!

I returned to deliver another presentation, and this time, instead of trussing myself in "corporate uniform," I wore a pair of jeans and a casual blouse. I sold forty-two policies! My words were unchanged and my products were the same. Curious about the radical tidal change, I asked them what was the deciding factor responsible for their business.

They told me they felt relaxed, found similarities in my background that made them feel comfortable and were generally more at ease in relating to me. I was not an authority figure in uniform, but one of them! Those few words sent my brain into a tailspin and taught me a vital lesson.

I began to test the theory and discovered that I had higher sales figures when I dressed in tune with my audience. From that point on, I applied this philosophy in every business endeavor and noticed it put people at ease, opened their minds and made them more receptive to me and my offerings! I was satisfied but not fulfilled, feeling this was not my final destination. I knew I had a long journey ahead and I still had to find the person I wanted to be.

A year later, Mutual of New York offered me the position of corporate sales trainer. I relocated to California for the job, but chose a different path to follow. I decided to get my masters degree, went to the University of Phoenix to enroll and was told by one of the advisors that I'd be a perfect candidate for the enrollment counselor position! I seized the opportunity and in just four weeks, I achieved top sales person status at the university! I had notoriety!

"Tonja, this is extraordinary! What are you doing to get this quota?" the sales manger said to me. I told him I was calling everyone I could and talking to them about their children enrolling and about the benefits of adults getting involved in continuing education programs. I made one appointment, scheduled everyone at the same time, gave my presentation, passed out enrollments slips and marched them directly to the bookstore.

Although success was gripping, I still felt a huge void. I was neither where I wanted to be nor who I wanted to be. I knew it was easy to make money when you enjoyed what you were doing. But I was sure real success arrives when you reach the happiest moment of your life. I knew I was not there yet and I knew that once again, it was time to move on!

1

The Way of Life of the Casual Millionaire

If you suddenly found yourself incredibly wealthy, would you continue doing what you're doing or would you immediately change the whole design of your life? Would you dress the same, continue to think as you do and maintain your general pattern of behavior—or would you empty your closets, resign from your job, demolish your house, divorce your spouse and totally renovate your whole life? If you opted for giving up what you're doing and abruptly interrupted your current routine, you're not happy being who you are and you're unmistakably miserably doing what you do!

Before I became the "casual millionaire," I was very much conditioned by a professional conformity code, which left me somewhat vulnerable regarding how I should dress in the business world. I wore suits and heels and adhered to a rather inflexible idea of what I was trained to believe was important, not what jazzed me. I attended meetings always in "corporate uniform" and eventually began to realize this was not the most productive way to conduct business. I often felt ill at ease in my surroundings and lacked the creative freedom I needed to become the person I designed myself to be.

On the other hand, the people I dealt with often shut down and pulled back, either unable or unwilling to relate to the stiff and conventional, corporate big-wig image I presented. This less than gratifying situation inspired me to take action. Fortunately, I had the ability to isolate the stepping stones and change the course of my journey.

Success is not about fancy dress or outdated protocol. It's about freedom and flexibility. It's about enhancing your life and channeling your thoughts into a powerhouse of energy that allows you to control how you will increase your income. It's about becoming wealthy doing what you love, comfortably and effortlessly.

However, if you're not there yet, there is a road map available to get you to your desired destination. You must program your mind to strive to get what you want and believe you will get it. The ability to change lies within every individual, but setting it in motion involves reprogramming your mind-set and fine-tuning your intentions to bring you in the right direction. If you're plagued with a fear of stepping out of your back yard and don't overcome the fear, it will be an impediment to your growing process. You cannot know how much greener the grass can be elsewhere unless you actually venture outside your little "safe and familiar play pen." If you are not willing to let go of the static and unproductive, you

will not be able to visit and explore new and promising terri-
tories. You have to relinquish all that hinders your progress,
learn to trust in change and begin, in faith and conviction, a
new journey.

Years ago, a *Great Gatsby* philosophy of abundance,
with flamboyant manifestations of financial opulence, represented the landscape of a millionaire lifestyle. People
were filthy rich and gloomy. The theme was either a "roaring twenties" self-indulgent, reckless and pretentious
flaunting of privileged status, or the rigid and formal
demeanor of *Gone with the Wind*—old wealth, girdled in
three piece suits and ties or pompous in Sunday hats, wrist
length white gloves and adorned with exorbitantly high-
priced jewels. An enviable picture perhaps, but all the
pomp and bling did not change the fact that millions of
dollars could not free these flashy individuals from the dic-
tates of how they should behave, what they should say and
how they should dress! All the abundance could not buy
them the freedom to be happy people, at ease with who
they were while enjoying the fruits of their labor. These
were millionaire marionettes, held firm by the strings of a
structured era.

Thankfully, it's no longer the "roaring twenties," and fortunately, no one wishes to emulate the lifestyle portrayed in
decades-old Hollywood films. This is a new century and with
it comes different ideas and the possibility to create from
your inner resources the life you would like to live. It's there
in the conscious, unconscious and higher intelligence you
come equipped with, but it's up to you to draw it out and
make it work for you.

The new millionaires' mantra is comfort and an unrestricted code of behavior. A casual attitude allows them to walk through a room filled with patrons in black tie and ball gowns and never realize they are dressed in jeans because they feel secure in their success, conscious of how much they have to offer and know they don't need to create an impression!

If given a pencil and a blank sheet of paper, how would you design your life? Can you express how it would feel? Can you explain how it would smell or describe what it would look like? If you know what it is you want but can't seem to get it, you need to pinpoint what or who is preventing you from achieving your objective. The secret is to gravitate towards the positive forces and away from the obstructive influences. A person who dotes on excusing his unhappy state by crying victim is simply reinforcing his position. This role is serving a purpose, even if a purely negative one. Channel the energy into letting go.

Many people I meet often tell me, "Tonja, change is so difficult. It's scary and so stressful."

To reassure them, I always find myself responding, "Why do you make it such a complicated task when in reality, change occurs in an instant?"

If you think about it, thirty-five-year chain smokers have broken the habit in the time it takes to extinguish a cigarette! This tells you that in order to live the casual millionaire lifestyle, you must put yourself in a position to make the appropriate decision to change the conditions and circumstances that are restricting you from achieving your goal. You have the power to judge your situation, evaluate the options and make the choices.

How you think influences what you will accomplish. You either build your own golden path with an easy, carefree passage to your destination or you set down an obstacle course filled with detours and dead end roads that lead nowhere! It's about you and the power of your intentions. Train your thoughts to assume positive outcomes. Positive affirmations bring optimism and constructive outcomes into your life. Restrictive beliefs do just that—they hamper and prevent you from reaching your destination. If you continue to trust the fact that money does not grow on trees, you will be shackled by your conviction. This type of silent brainwashing remains trapped in the subconscious, expanding in time and manifesting itself in a lacking and limited lifestyle.

In my seminars, I always tell people that in my house, contrary to popular belief, money does grow on trees. And to cancel out the limiting idea instilled in me from childhood, I took $5, $10, $20 and $50 bills and hung them with clothespins on a plant in the corner of my room. Whenever I pass my "money tree," I reassure myself that in my house, money does grow on trees!

As children we were unable to set our intentions because they were pretty much locked into our heads, but as adults, we can reprogram our subconscious minds to delete the negative worms that cause the system to break down. Learn to monitor your own potential-limiting thoughts and start training your conscious mind to get what you want instead of dwelling on what you have or don't have. Cut the poisonous verbiage—rewrite your inner dictionary to substitute "I can't" with "I can" and "I will." Pay careful attention to your thoughts in order to cancel what will hold you back. Train your thoughts to get what you want, and don't take no for an answer.

You believe it's only in the mind until one day when you discover that what you think about is exactly what you bring about. Suddenly, your dreams become your reality. Then you move a step further and notice that what you focus on expands! These few simple words equate to a successful motivational tool, dependent exclusively on your own interior resources for energy!

The mind is a very potent vehicle and if properly driven, it will lead you directly to your destination. Therefore, if wealth and abundance are the objective of your journey, you need to fuel your energy with positive intentions. Accepting as reality that what you think about is what you bring about and what you focus on expands, will motivate you to take control of your life. Often, I call to mind the very pertinent and wise words of Mahatma Gandhi: "A man is but the product of his thoughts—what he thinks, he becomes." In essence, you have within you all the resources needed to control and maybe it's time to surpass outdated and outgrown concepts that hinder your journey.

The casual millionaire way of life is not about laid-back responsibility, lack of accountability or neglecting your investments. Neither is it about trashing the laws of prosperity. Instead, in order to enjoy that casual life, it is necessary to educate and train yourself to learn how to keep reaching your objectives. It's about dropping the negativity to make space for positive creativity. Most people don't realize that they hold the power within themselves to become greater individuals simply because this idea is in contradiction with years of indoctrination that created a limited-potential mental picture of who they are. This narrow-vision tendency, in time, becomes a bad second nature, like a bad habit. These habits are the result of conditioning, and though sometimes not easy to rectify, they can be broken!

Personally, I rid my mind of unconstructiveness by refusing to watch news broadcasts or read the daily newspapers! People laugh at me and ask, "Tonja, how can you stay on top of the real estate market if you don't follow the media reports?" In response, I just smile and tell them that because I'm not filling my mind with media reporting, the real estate market exists as I design it in my world! This media separation liberates me from the entanglements, one-sided conditioning and sometimes complicated issues my colleagues are forced to deal with. I believe that if I should be tuned in to something important, the message will be delivered to my ears. In one way or another, some well-informed individual who watches and reads will come along, and I will be told what I need to know without having to cram my mind with all the negativity in the universe!

A number of years ago, Anne Murray had a song titled, "A Little Good News." The lyrics referenced Bryant Grumble's piece on the fighting in Lebanon. Her simple but powerful words—"Just once how I'd like to see the headlines say, 'Not much to print today, can't find nothin' bad to say.' We sure could use a little good news today"—centered on hearing some good things just once, and they impacted my life. I decided I too wanted to set only positive intentions and would block out the pessimistic things and circumstances that served exclusively to thwart my course to the finish line.

I disciplined myself to isolate and eliminate the negative forces and influences that bind, because to live the causal millionaire lifestyle, you need to be energized with positive power, to move forward and satisfy your expectations. You'll accomplish much more in a day, easily and effortlessly, since you are in the flow of being at ease with the person you are and in the surge of your own positive energy. In essence, you are situated in the flow of doing what you love and loving what you do. At this point you automatically attain the results you set your intention on achieving.

A couple of years ago, I spent some time reading poems I had written as a child. I was surprised by the deep spiritual vein as well as the colorful imagery that ran through the verses. My thoughts brought me back to that era and I recalled how my mom would encourage me to dream and visualize all the things I wanted to be and do with my life. At the time, I had no idea how powerful this creative process I was using to design my life actually was in helping me get what I wanted and where I desired to go.

I also learned that there were people who always talked about what they were going to do but never made a move, accomplishing little, and conversely, there were others who remained silent but met all their expectations in the end. I concluded there was a phenomenal power in silence, in not releasing your dreams and goals into the universe, keeping the energy potent. Talking consumes energy. If you tell your plans, you risk having people try to convince you that your ideas are unproductive or just ridiculous. Envy prohibits others from wanting you to be one step ahead of the game. Envy discourages and destroys, never builds or supports.

However, I consider myself very fortunate because my mom spent her life encouraging me to develop an inner awareness and teaching me the value of responsibility and accountability in achieving success. She told me there are two ways to perceive any given situation, just like there are two sides to every coin: heads and tails. You can either be happy or sad, successful or a failure. And although you are in control, you are obliged to select wisely because your choice will have a definite effect on you, bringing either positive results or potentially serious repercussions.

Mom also told me, whenever I was upset with her and threatening to withhold my words to "punish" her, that I would pay the penalty, not her. I questioned this affirmation, believing my silent treatment would cause her to suffer. Instead, she explained how my foolish decision would be harmful only to me. I was the one who would waste time walking around angry and filled with heavy resentment. Carrying all this negative baggage would serve only to deplete the energy I could have channeled into a productive endeavor. In the end, all I accrued was a forfeited opportunity to attain a goal.

Now, I think of my day in terms of a financial energy bank. I start with a million dollars worth of energy units. I calculate how much it "costs" me, based on energy units, to speak with each person who engages me in a conversation. At the end of the day, I either increase my "bank account" or decrease it as a result of my encounters. Some people's energy fields are draining because they detract from your life, siphon your energy and leave you depleted. On the other hand, some people enhance your life and productivity, and add to your energy account. It's important to plan wisely and decide how you want to spend your energy units in a way that will profit you and make you feel good about yourself. Be selective about what you put on your plate instead of just piling on and creating a chaotic, tasteless mess. In the end, what's on your plate is what you have to swallow.

The casual millionaire lifestyle is about giving your best performance while enjoying the show you're creating. It's about sculpting your own days and evenings to fit your wishes, needs and inclinations. The wealth accumulated doing what you love is about time and freedom—time to do whatever you want, whenever you want to and with whomever you want. Financial elasticity eliminates concern over bills due and credit card debt. Economic flexibility allows you to be confident-casual with yourself and gives you the ability and possibility to turn an ideal life of abundance and contentment into a real life of affluence and fulfillment—yours!

2

Self-Appraisal & Personal Appreciation

You can choose to be either your greatest asset or your most lethal liability. This is the power you hold over your net worth—a power that originates in your mind. You can put yourself in a position to reap abundance if you take the time to determine your strengths and weaknesses, and define not only what you want but what you don't want. Human nature has a tendency to fall back on negative thinking, especially in younger years. However, part of the growing process involves objectively identifying who you are and digging to the root of your thoughts with an open and honest mind.

I discovered that many people who come through my training seminars assure me they want to be multi-millionaires. They speak with conviction and certainty, yet in essence, what they are really looking for is financial security. There is a large dividing wall between serenely enjoying the comforts of life and having multi-millions of dollars. The first situation is ideal for individuals who don't want to be concerned about due bills and fast-accruing credit card debt, but are not willing to assume the responsibility attached to a multi-millionaire status. Having enormous wealth carries serious challenges, such as the constant movement of money. Before a decision is made, it is essential to take personal inventory and objectively clarify the things you say you want versus the things you really want!

Stop and think for a moment. Ask yourself what it would take to become a millionaire. Then go a step further and question what it would take to defend and maintain your position, once you've accumulated great wealth. Are you ready to commit to the responsibilities associated with your new abundance, and is this new game plan what you really want in your life at this time?

Many people coveting big fortunes fail to realize that the tightest string attached to having a lot of money is accountability. Enjoying the spending power and freedom from *want,* associated with having more than enough money does not equate with assuming the full responsibility of managing a multi-millionaire status. There is a very strong line separating the two positions. Here, once again, it is important to determine if you truly want to achieve millionaire status. And, should the answer be no, then ask yourself, what is it you want? Perhaps you dream of having an extra $30,000 added to your annual earnings and are willing to do whatever it takes to get this increase. Maybe this is as far as you're willing to commit, and possibly this is the essential component of your wishful thinking. In other words, the extra 30 thousand is the objective of your dream, and achieving this goal will give you the power and tranquility you wish.

Besides defining what you want, it is also essential to establish what you don't want. This can be tricky and somewhat challenging to understand because it entails extracting from all the things you say you don't want, the things you actually want. At first, it sounds like a brainteaser, but thinking about it, you realize that at some level there is a desire, conscious or otherwise, for what you are getting in your life. Franklin Roosevelt understood the concept of the mind's power over destiny and would frequently say, "Men are not prisoners of fate, but prisoners of their own mind." His words ring true, since you live the life you create. Whether you realize it or not, you actually have what you want.

And whether you are aware of it or not, you manifest your deepest wants and desires, which keep appearing until you not only make the decision to change them, but act on your resolution. It's an interesting concept to explore. Once you start focusing your attention on discovering the reason why what you say you don't want continues to reappear, you'll find yourself in the role of Columbo, haggling and probing for answers. Eventually, you'll discover things appear because you give them "permission" to appear—after you have identified what you want, decide why you want it, and in what part of your life you want it to materialize.

If you want the wild flowers that restrict you from attaining your objectives to disappear, weed out the garden and plant new seeds. This is the only way you can start to grow lush blooms. It is a process of discovery, elimination and replanting new intentions, which will help you redevelop and redesign who you are and where you're going.

I always equate the growing process with kids, because they offer proof that determining what you want is far more complex than it seems. If you ask high school students what careers they will choose as adults, most will respond with seven or eight ideas. The same question posed to college freshmen will bring more focused answers, even though the possibilities may still be varied. As seniors, they have it narrowed down, usually to two or three options. Later, with MD or JD degrees tucked under their arms, when asked if they are going to be doctors or lawyers, you may get a "Well, I think so" response. The truth is, they went through years of study, have all the credentials and the letters after their names, yet once they have stepped into their professional roles, they suddenly realize the profession they have chosen is not what they thought it would be or what they expected! The disappointment occurred as a result of not envisioning what being a lawyer or doctor entailed. They did not have a mental picture of themselves in that specific role.

It's important to learn that you create and become what you are able to perceive. On the other hand, what you cannot visualize, you will neither become nor accomplish. Projection is a key segment of your journey. Train yourself to visualize whom you to want to be and what you want to become. Then, observe yourself in the situation you have designed in your mind. Read the script and play the part!

Participate in your vision. Try on the suit of the attorney, step into the scrubs of the surgeon and determine how you feel. How does walking in the shoes of a multi-millionaire resonate with you? In other words, act out your own dream—don't just sit on the sidelines watching others become successful. Be a willing accomplice.

Nobody develops a golden tan from the word "sun"! If you don't open yourself to it, if you don't allow the rays to penetrate your skin, if you're not fully involved in the process, you will not reap the benefits.

When I was a high school student, there were one or two people who walked around dressed in suits, carrying brief cases. One guy in particular always remained in my mind. His name was Charles, and he always showed up for class impeccably dressed in the garb of a successful businessman. Today, he is the CEO of a Fortune 500 company!

I'm convinced Charles achieved his objective because he prepared himself for his thriving career early in life. He took all the flak from the other kids for his rather pompous way of dressing but let it roll off, visualizing himself at a young age as an accomplished professional. Charles stepped into the role he designed for himself. This was the identity he created, and he was determined to wear the "uniform" of success, despite the consequences. He was accountable for his choices, which as I remember were the result of conscious planning. Thinking back, I often smile to myself, because at the time, my primary concern was just getting out of high school!

Projection is somewhat of a dress rehearsal, a kind of dry run that permits you to imagine how you feel on that particular stage. Running through the scenario in your mind will allow you to question if you feel uncomfortable with the liability your role presents, if you're willing to accept the responsibility or if the accountability suits your intention. If you don't give yourself a standing ovation, you have the opportunity to rewrite the scene to fit your needs, wants and expectations.

I find it helpful to make a list and jot down all the circumstances that make you feel uncomfortable or unproductive. Then, utilize the input and work on determining how you can substitute the negative conditions with positive situations that make you feel good about yourself, and more importantly, put you in a position to contribute something to others. Contribution has a magnetic pull. Everyone has a strong desire to donate a "piece" of themselves to the world, to give part of the gifts they have received. Teachers do it teaching, preachers preaching and successful people, motivating—all for the good of others.

However, if you feel that what you are doing doesn't set you in a position to make a difference, then chances are it's not worth doing. Knowing you're a contributor to the overall scheme of the universe opens you to the enjoyment of personal gratification. Once this "feeling good" comes into focus, you can turn the activity that created the inspirational emotion into an income-producing tool. This will enhance your journey and move you closer to your desired destination.

Often, I see people entangled in an "I've got to make money" web. They are caught up in the stacks of bills to be paid and pushed into hysteria by the "I've got to be somebody" hype that equates with success. My take on this modern day "frenzy" is that you don't have to struggle to be somebody, you are already somebody! The question is, how do you want to shine your "big-wig" sign? And in what direction do you want to send your contribution?

I remember spending a great part of my life trying to be somebody. I was determined to be a corporate VIP, to jump into and invade that identity. Then I realized that the minute I released the idea of being the major player, I actually became the person I was meant to become.

Positive affirmations and incantations exercise a distinctive influence on becoming who you're designed to be. You have to talk to yourself graciously, because most people don't speak to you amiably. So if you don't give yourself this respect, no one else will. People sometimes laugh at me because it seems as if I'm mentally dysfunctional. I walk around and consciously engage myself in conversation, pronouncing affirming words. If you pass me on the street or in a shop, chances are you'll hear me say, "Money flows into my life easily and effortlessly. I respect, honor and cherish money and therefore money shows up for me in ways I've never even imagined or dreamed!"

Money comes down the path I envisioned it to travel along, as well as in other surprising ways. It shows up in my universe because money "knows," and the energy of money "knows" I'm committed to cherishing, supporting and taking care of it. Money also "knows" I'm willing to look after and care for the planet. As Whitman said, "When I give, I give myself."

If I'm looking for a new opportunity, I focus on this intention through the power of my spoken word, directed to myself and to the universe instead of to other individuals. While I'm getting dressed in the morning, I'll borrow some of the chants I learned from Tom Hopkins in a sales training class, and select what is appropriate to satisfy my need in a particular moment. One of my favorites—"I'm alive, I'm awake and I feel great"—is a wonderful self-greeting at the start of a new day.

Frequently, I add my own words to my morning chants, depending upon my daily objective and how I'm feeling. If I awaken sluggish, I'll pump myself up by saying things that reassure me I'm in control of my physiological state as well as my mental and emotional conditions. The more energy you accrue in your body, the greater ability you have to create, as you're actually using the momentum and the energy to get things rolling. If you ever wondered why the busiest people on the planet have the highest accomplishment quotient, this will answer your question!

Observing my staff in the office, I'm able to isolate the employee whose "busy factor" is not as high as the others. I also know that if I want something accomplished, I have to entrust the job to the person who takes on the most. It seems like a vicious cycle, but those who work get things done and therefore always have something to do.

Getting back to the self-conversation, I want to emphasize the importance of being kind to yourself, being motivational, being inspirational and being demanding. Challenge yourself to go "forward and up," to meet a new standard. In my lectures, I often refer to my "step up" motto—decide where your next level will be, then step up to it, step up into it and show up to step up! You begin this part of your journey carrying the entire person you are, in order to get into whatever you want to get into. Go forward and courageously step on to higher ground, refusing today the mediocrity you may have accepted from yourself yesterday.

I believe everyone knows when they are settling—when they accept a given situation or set of conditions, fully aware that they are capable of a greater outcome. When you are certain you can accomplish more but choose not to, in reality you are not the author of this process of selection. Instead, you are relinquishing your intention, stepping back and putting yourself in a position to be guided by outside forces. This course of action serves to generate an undercurrent of shame, which drains the energy out of life. Avoid shame and its all-consuming effects. Take responsibility; be conscious of the fact that this is your choice exclusively. You will fall into it neither blindly nor compromisingly, and as a result of your decision, you will not allow shame to wreak havoc in your life.

I cannot stop emphasizing the potency of positive affirmations and incantations, which involve fueling your mind with productive energy. Last month, I said to a woman who participated in one of my seminars, "It's not sufficient to get excited. You need to inhale your enthusiasm, summon it up, work it and experience it! Wear your passions on your facial expressions. Manifest them with your body language. Be alive and enchanted with the magic of excitation! If you don't allow the excitement to take full possession of you, the words you say become meaningless and powerless, simply because the sound of your voice projects one message and your physiology another. Perk up your smile and fine-tune your laugh! Give a 'living' sign of life."

I wanted to motivate her to treat her vital energy as a

priceless bottle of Mouton Rothschild and decant it into her body. I encouraged her to live life. She responded by saying, "Tonja, it's so hard because I have not done that in such a long time." I reassured her it was not as difficult as she was visualizing it in her mind. Basically, it takes one action—getting rid of those embarrassment-producing thoughts and fears that impede you from showing your feelings. Jump for joy, demonstrate your excitement and vocalize it. Forget the schooling that taught you to melt into the background, silence your passions and try to pass up the occasion to humiliate yourself by uncorking your feelings in public. Let it out before you burst the bubble.

I told her, "Are you nuts, holding it all in? Just pretend no one is around. Go home and do it. Start on a small scale and get comfortable with expressing your feelings!"

Several weeks later, she came to another seminar. I noticed how uplifted she looked. She was totally "renovated"!

"Oh my God, Tonja," she said. "I'm running around my house, yelling out these affirmations in front of the mirror. I'm laughing and smiling and having a ball. My family thinks I'm nuts!"

"Well," I responded, "you are nuts. You're nuts because for so many years, you lived your life the way somebody else told you it needed to be lived, and you couldn't even express this vibrancy expanding within you!" No one has the right to choreograph your life, primarily because no one knows you as well as you know yourself.

Feelings, thoughts and ideas must be channeled out of the body and turned into actions in order to have life. Let them out! Who cares what anyone thinks. The opinions of others should matter little. If you feel good and inspired walking around the house singing and laughing, do it. You don't need to be a Grammy-winning singer. Just open your mouth and sing! This is a self-nurturing process that cancels out the "What is everyone else thinking about me?" philosophy that suffocates creativity. It liberates!

This personal freedom leads to financial independence, abundance and prosperity. It's about dedication and "smart" work as opposed to just "hard" work! If you do a self-appraisal, you will be in a position to make a "tear-down trait" in your character appreciate into a lucrative "turn key" asset! As I mentioned previously, it's a journey—a "passage" that involves exposing the parts and aspects of your being that can help you achieve your true autonomy, personally and professionally.

This process does not have to be based solely on your own experiences. Contrary to what you've been told, experience is not the best teacher! If you're obliged to sail through life experiencing everything first hand, you'll be a centenarian before you're "educated" or wise enough to stand on your own two feet. Instead, be able to calculate the value of listening. Employ a positive attitude to affirm your capabilities. If necessary, redevelop and redesign who you are. Educate yourself: let the experiences of others sketch your own "floor plan" to success.

I'd like to share my own personal experience, which I believe demonstrates the power of positive thinking. When I was a young child, about nine or ten years told, I used to walk around saying, "I want to be dirty, rotten, filthy, stinking rich!" These were my exact words. Analyzing the choice of words I used to enhance rich, you will realize how offbeat my idea of having abundant wealth was. Actually, a Cab Calloway song titled "I Wanna Be Rich" triggered my brain into composing my own lyrics! I remember it had a great beat but not a very congenial concept of being wealthy. Every time I played the song, I sang along, changing his, "Cash cold that's what I need…I wanna be rich" lyrics to, "I want to be dirty, rotten, filthy stinking, rich!" I was literally obsessed with this phrase; I even put it on a button and pinned it on my clothes.

All through high school and even during my ten year, ten month and ten day career in the Air Force, I kept the button among my possessions in a little junk box of memorabilia. I remember picking it up one day and realizing that what I had inscribed on the button, I had actually manifested in my life, because in reality I was dirty, rotten, filthy, stinking rich. Translation: I was flat broke!

In the military, I had earned less than $20,000 a year, yet churning in my mind was the idea that I was going to be rich. I knew that if I was going to be wealthy, I was in the wrong place. The Air Force would only allow me so much room for financial growth, and I was certain that if I remained, I would never achieve my objective. Second, I realized that my mindset, which defined rich as dirty, rotten, filthy and stinking, was not going to work, since it dug into a belief system that gave money a polluted face—and attributed a rotten, nasty nature to being affluent!

One afternoon, I looked at the button for the last time. I remember thinking I would never become rich if I continued to give a negative character to wealth by repeatedly chanting this phrase. I knew it was time to throw away the button, along with my faulty opinion. This enlightening moment triggered the realization that marked a turning point in my life.

I rebooted my mindset, developed a philosophical conviction for religious science and started reading more about Ernest Homes, Maryann Williamson, Wayne Dyer and Dr. Deepak Chopra, familiarizing myself with their ideas, viewpoints, perspectives and belief systems. Reading their books, I noticed that the common thread flowing through their philosophies was related to my own thoughts and thinking. In fact, this was similar to everything my mom had taught me while growing up.

As a young woman, I started to imagine how I could take all this great advice I had accumulated and use it to make a positive difference in my life. I knew I had to make the decision to get rid of those pessimistic words. They were obstructing my journey and holding me back from achieving my objective. I knew I had to restructure my thought processes. That call to action marked the end of dirty, rotten, filthy, stinking rich. From that moment forward, whenever I caught myself reciting my old mantra, I would stop and replace the negative words with, "I'm going to be the most pleasant, most powerful, wealthiest person who does good on the planet. This will affect my life in a positive way, because being wealthy means happiness." This was my mantra. My thoughts were now aligned with my wishes, and I was sure this harmonious balance would help me get what I wanted.

Soon after, on Thanksgiving Day, I had run over to Albertson's to pick up something I had forgotten. Walking

towards the entry, I noticed a shiny penny lying on the
ground. It glittered in the sunlight. I glanced at it about
twenty times, raising and lowering my eyes while I debated
with myself whether or not I should lean over and make it
mine. Running through my mind were the words, "Pick it
up, pick it up." Simultaneously, running counter clockwise
were the words, "It's just a penny, let it go."

As a child, I would pick up every penny I found, make a
wish and put it in my left shoe. However, at the store, I did
not have a cart; therefore, my hands were overloaded with
packages. I ping-ponged from, "Is it worth it to inconven-
ience myself and put down all my bags for a penny?" to my
original, "Pick it up." I wrestled for several moments between
the two alternatives and finally said out loud, "Alright,
alright, I'm picking it up!" I took a deep breath, set all my
groceries down, snatched the penny and slipped it into my
pocket.

As I reached for my packages, I heard a voice from
behind: "Honey, that's prosperity," a woman said. I glanced
at her and she continued, "I'm snickering because I heard you
arguing with yourself. If you respect money, you'll get more
of it—because how can you expect the universe to give you
$200 if you can't pick up a penny?" I was taught a very
important lesson that day—I learned that even a penny has
value in the grand scheme of life.

My experiences have been filled with valuable learning
possibilities, but in order to reap from the daily circumstances, it takes an open mind. Another little incident that
may at first seem meaningless resulted in a new, essential life
lesson.

One day, shortly before I started my first business, I had decided to spend some time relaxing at Laguna Beach. My hands were overloaded with books and I noticed the city had just changed the parking system from a coin-operated machine to one that worked with tickets. Expecting to deal with the nickel, dime and quarter machine, I had only loose change in my wallet. I realized this would not be acceptable for the updated system. I walked over to the machine just to verify if it had a slot for coins. It didn't!

From the corner of my eye, I noticed a couple approaching me. "We're leaving," the woman said, "and we have two hours left on our ticket." She extended her arm, adding, "Here, the ticket is yours!"

Unhesitatingly I responded, "Oh no—I can pay you for it, if you don't mind taking it in coins. I don't have any money with me."

"No, no," she responded, "this is a gift."

I held fast to my wanting to pay for it and she was insistent upon refusing my money. Several moments later, she turned to me and said, "You've got to learn to receive." She gazed down at my hands, pointed her finger at one of the books I was carrying and said, "I see you're reading *The Millionaire Next Door.* I'm offering you a gift. Stop fighting it. Take it and learn to say thank you. Thank you are the best words you can ever say to anyone."

I looked at her, smiled, said a gracious thank you and went about my business. That day at Laguna Beach, I had received another essential life lesson.

It was amazing how several individuals in everyday situations played major roles in helping me evaluate and remodel my mindset in order to change my thought process into an asset producing "investment". I learned about the laws of prosperity and how my own thinking factored into the equation. I understood I was not off track in considering the importance of thinking. If a handful of strangers were able to catch my faulty thought patterns and obviously felt I was struggling with diverse issues, I knew it was not enough to just set new intentions; I had to act upon them if I wanted to accomplish my objectives.

Initially, I spoke about giving and making contributions, all of which place you in a position to receive. This is an essential part of prosperity. And when you are an open vessel, ready and agreeable to receiving instead of repeatedly spending your energy building barriers to lock out what's given, you will receive more from the universe. Many people, willing or otherwise, are their own snags to prosperity.

If someone compliments you, accept it graciously with a smile and a sincere acknowledgement of thanks, instead of debating the giver's judgment. If you're told you look good, chances are you don't look like a monster! Don't rebut with condescending comments: "Oh, I didn't sleep well, I have a horrific face." This display of insecurity serves only to detour your journey towards achieving your objectives.

When you have the opportunity to receive, you create a very special environment. In receiving the compliment, both parties gain benefits. The giver is not dismissed and feels good having made someone's day shine, whereas the recipient gets to fully receive the kind deed in the power and presence of that unique moment of synergy.

Words of gratitude and giving words of praise are important

vehicles. If you know you're a fantastic attorney, admit it—
accept it! When you deny or refuse your positive qualities or
accomplishments, you halt the flow and impede the recogni-
tion of virtue. It's not about bragging. Make a treasure of the
wise words of Nelson Mandela:

> "Our deepest fear is not that we are inade-
> quate...but powerful beyond measure. We ask
> ourselves, who am I to be brilliant, gorgeous, tal-
> ented and famous? Actually, who are you not to
> be? You are a child of God. Your playing small
> does not serve the world!"

In essence, being who you are and acknowledging what
you do helps elevate the level of achievement in the universe.
Letting your own light glow encourages others to let theirs
shine. It gives people permission to openly discuss their
achievements. Some individuals feel that talking about their
accomplishments may sadden or discourage those who have
not quite made it yet. However, what they fail to realize is
that success stories motivate and plant the seeds of hope.
Wealth is not just a figment of the imagination. Wealth is a
reality!

Others fear envy or bad karma and refuse to share accomplishments, believing that, as the Italians say, *per scaramanzia*
(to not jinx it), it is best to keep your triumphs locked in a
safety-net of silence! After the fact, it's broadcast to the four
corners of the world. I think it's best to just put it out there—
share it; give it back to the universe!

Personally, I trust my Higher Power. During my
moments of meditation, I share. And in my role as teacher

and motivational speaker, I also share, illustrating my ideas
and philosophies with examples from my life to enable others
to identify with my journey. However, I am also cautious,
because not knowing everyone in my audience, I often tend
to wrap a protective energy field around myself. This does
not stop me from reaching out to all those who attend my
seminars and lectures, because witnessing others grow,
become assertive and live their intentions through my sharing, is a phenomenal payback! After all, "playing small" may
not serve the world, but "playing big" certainly does!

3
Location! Location! Location!

To be successful, it is essential to discover what you like to do, because what you enjoy doing and what you do naturally, using your talents, becomes the groundwork for achievements. Center on finding your own niche, that potentially lucrative location from where you will be able to develop and invest the talents you have.

Your endowments and special aptitudes will manifest themselves in what you are interested in doing. For example, if you're fascinated with the medical world, chances are you have an aptitude for science and are a service-oriented person. On the other hand, if math was not your best subject as a student, don't aspire to become an accountant. You will be unhappy and not give your best performance. Instead, let your talents and the fields in which you excel be your guide. If you follow your inclinations, you will be happy, and being happy and liking what you do sets you on a path for success. "Real success is finding your life work in the work that you love." This wise thought, expressed by David McCullough, serves to reinforce my own personal theory.

Success is not about choosing a career or a profession; it's not about getting a job. It's about locating your strengths and identifying your true desires. It's about isolating your weaknesses and not repeating faulty decisions. Essentially, it's about uncovering what makes you feel good about yourself and what makes you comfortable enough to shine your brightest light. More importantly, it's about asking yourself what you really want to do and determining how you can work to your full potential for a positive outcome.

I firmly believe that everyone has a special treasure in the gifts they have received. However, these talents need to be developed and utilized in order to render them effective. We awaken each morning noticing a distinctive pull towards a given activity. We know with certainty we can spend an entire day doing this, be content and feel gratified. However, outside influences such as the media, teachers, parents and peers often impede us from following our natural instincts.

From early on, as young children, we're inoculated with ideas that certain career and professional choices are tickets to wealth, if not outright fame and fortune! I remember my parents telling me, "Tonja, doctors make a lot of money!" Well, from where I stand today, I don't believe one can generalize this consideration, because in reality, most physicians don't take home the big bucks they have a reputation for earning!

There are stereotyped professions presented to children. They are glamorized and "marketed" with promises of becoming rich. No thought is spent on a child's capabilities or desires. What they like to do and what they are good at doesn't enter into the decision, yet these factors are the stepping-stones to success. When kids choose, they base their selections on criteria that does not equate with who they are, what they like and what they are good at. Instead, they use the often misleading "big bucks" principle as a decisive factor. This is a recipe for a lifetime of professional dissatisfaction and non-productivity, especially if they persevere, fearful of change.

I'll share a recent experience that I think emphasizes my point quite clearly. Recently, I hired a new office assistant who came to my company and applied for the job. This 21-year-old woman had absolutely no administrative skills, no discernment and little if any capability to think forward or project herself into the position. Her inability to perform the tasks required was not a consequence of her young age and inexperience; it was a question of mistaken talent identity. In other words, she was not geared to be an administrative assistant and her career choice demonstrated she had not yet taken the time to either understand whom she was or pinpoint her correct location. Since she was not doing what she was good at, she was misplaced and not where she should have been, which was that distinctive location where she would excel.

Observing her around the office, I discovered that this young woman had a talent for listening and was able to generate initiatives as soon as a project idea came into focus. She offered advice, volunteered helpful suggestions and was a willing and enthusiastic participant. However, she had channeled her energy down the wrong path, believing it would be a learning experience. It was, in a sense, because she now knows her erroneous choice would never have allowed her to develop her abilities and would certainly not bring out the best in her. She had a way to go before she would be familiar and comfortable enough with her sense of self to veer in the direction that would eventually lead her to peak performance.

As soon as I spotted this bad-fit career option, I pulled her out and told her, "Listen, this is not going to work—we have to get you out of it. What will work is to find something that will let you put your talents to profitable use. Something that feels natural and that you love doing! And something that integrates your interests and capabilities, turning them into valuable assets!"

I knew she had a lot of exploring to do, since she was obviously treading along a beaten path. Although it was a vital part of her journey, it gave her proof she was still lost to herself. However, if she wanted to uncover her true self, I advised her to think and probe outside of the pre-established *milieu* everyone else determined would be a suitable career environment for her. It was crucial to choose a path she could feel comfortable traveling along, and essential to realize the worthlessness of "going with the flow" just because she was influenced by the opinions and or experiences of others. I think Oprah Winfrey hit the target when she said, "I've come to believe that each of us has a personal calling that is as unique as a fingerprint—and that the best way to succeed is to discover what you love!"

Often, people approach me during my seminars and ask, "Tonja, you talk about discovering who you are and what you want to become—well that sounds fine, but how do I find myself? What do I have to do?"

As a response, I often share an experience from my own life that I feel gives a concrete example and is perhaps easy for others to relate to. Usually, I like to go back to my initial years in the military, because it was a time dedicated to soul searching, groping for answers, investigating options and trying to decipher who I was, what I wanted and where I should be to attain my intentions.

My very first assignment in the Air Force was in the supply squadron. To be more precise, I worked in inventory management. I was 18 years old and my job description entailed utilizing a huge machine to literally pull carbon out of paper for the purpose of creating reports. The task lacked both creativity and originality, and it was tedious and excruciatingly boring! As a result, my performance was beyond mediocre: I was awful. My attention to detail was non-existent, my interest level rated a subzero and my concentration had a lifespan of less than a minute.

One day, exasperated from the tedious carbon-pulling chore, I thought to myself, "Is this going to be my life?" I answered my own question, admitting to myself, "I'm just not good at this. No, actually I'm terrible! I stink at it!" It's neither easy nor gratifying to acknowledge your failings, but denying flaws will not allow room for corrections or improvement. Consequently, instead of improving, you stagnate.

Fortunately, I had a rather opportune learning experience. I was open-minded and receptive to acquiring the knowledge I needed to get me where I intended to go. I recall the afternoon my mentor approached me after work. Obviously aware I was not delighted both with my job and with my actual performance, he confronted me, asking, "Tonja, how do you like this job?"

I was truthful when I responded, "This is not what I envision myself doing."

His rebuttal was, "Well, Tonja, then why are you so bad at it?"

He caught me by surprise and I blurted, "What do you mean by that?"

He responded, "Get good at everything you do!"

His line of thinking forced me to reconsider what I was doing, why my performance level was so deficient, where I wanted to go from here and how I would get to my desired destination.

Today, many years later, I can still hear my mentor's wise words: "Tonja, when you get good at what you're doing, you can write your own ticket to another destination! You can choose what you want to do and with whom you want to do it. If you don't like pulling carbon, if you find it boring and not challenging enough, get better at it. Once you're a master at what you're doing, your hiring potential is elevated. Everyone will seek to employ you for whatever job you choose. "

Basically, his advice made sense. Success moves you forward while failure traps you, preventing you from reaching our destination. If I wanted to continue my journey, I knew I had to excel at pulling carbon from paper, regardless of the monotony and superlative boredom factor.

I found my mentor's words both amazing and enlightening. I knew I had to "locate myself"—differentiate between what I had a natural talent for and loved doing, and what I did because I was assigned to. It was part of the process. But, I had to make the decision to act on my inclinations. It was obvious I was in the wrong location and had to relocate. In so doing, I had to reprogram my mindset and learn that choice was all about creating my own design!

I began to scout for my new location by listening to some of the good advice from qualified people around me, even though the suggestions were not necessarily directed towards me. I also began to explore what I liked about everything I became involved in. When I decided to give my best performance in whatever I did, regardless of the price I had to pay, I was able to distinguish between what I really enjoyed doing and excelled at because I was working with a natural talent, and what I was deficient in. When boredom replaces motivation, you are unable to determine your productivity quotient, which tells you how good or bad you are at a specific job. You can only identify what you want to do and conversely what you absolutely don't want to do!

There is a major diversity between what you're good at and what you enjoy doing. And although the two aspects differ, they are connected in the master plan of life. Therefore, it is necessary to find the link.

Getting back to my own process of discovery, I'll mention that I realized I had actually enjoyed going through basic training. The discipline was edifying, I loved the marching, the drills were exciting and the outdoor environment was invigorating. Moving about from place to place was exciting. It captivated my interest, stimulated my energy source and lengthened my attention span. It was motivating!

One day, I picked up a copy of *Airmen's Magazine* and flipping through it, I came across an insert advertising for female military training instructors. It immediately caught my attention. I projected myself into the position and actually heard my voice say, "I can teach." Although I had never been involved in teaching, was never advised or outwardly told to follow that career path, I felt I had the capability to do it. I just knew it was the right place for me at that time.

Convinced I could do it, I applied for the position and became a training instructor. Soon after, I had the confirmation my intuition was right on target and the affirmation I had made the correct choice. I was where I should be. However, in order to find my perfect space, I had to step into and preview many diverse locations. I remember that all through the journey, one stubbornly persistent thought kept surfacing" "God, I'm just not good at this. Am I ever going to be successful?"

I hold firm to my belief that life is a process of choices. Everything you create and design is powered by choice. However, it is important to separate rendering a decision from making a choice. Where you are and what you do can either be determined by choice or left to a decision. The "God does not play dice" metaphor expressed by Einstein, lays bare the discrepancy. If you decide to entrust your career option to others, be they guidance counselors, teachers, business coaches or mentors, your throw of the dice will not necessarily guarantee success because in reality, you are not choosing what you want to do or where you want to be professionally. Someone else takes the initiative to relocate you!

However, if being successful doing what you love doing and using and developing your natural talents is your game, then move forward—step up and choose it. Plant the choice to make that choice in your subconscious, and then act on it. I think Wayne Dyer hit the bulls' eye when he said, "Be miserable. Or motivate yourself. Whatever has to be done, it's always your choice!"

4

Setting Your
Intention

Intention is your most potent tool! When properly utilized, it impregnates the mind with valuable ideas and thoughts. It maps out your journey, sets your pace and charts your direction. In other words, intention is the "pulse" of your mind, the life force that changes it from a blank page to a thriving font of resources. Without it, your mind would be an empty space—useless.

The power of intention is the energy that actually empowers you. It is, in essence, the merger between wish and resolve. Desiring something doesn't come with a guarantee for attaining it, unless you program your will towards moving forward to get it.

I like to think of intention as the clout behind the throne, the influential factor that determines if your choice will be successful or not! Sometimes people ask me, "Tonja, how do intentions differ from goals?"

I tell them, "Your goals are indispensable. Their purpose is to serve as a 'to do' list, itemizing your desired accomplishments. For instance, you may want get a graduate degree or aspire to sell a million-dollar house. However, what really makes it happen—what pushes your goal off the 'to do' list and into a positive outcome, is your intention! These thoughts that invade the consciousness have more startling effects on the nature of your outcomes than you often realize."

I remember setting my intentions before I acquired a clear definition of what I was doing. Looking back, I realize it was something I did automatically. Now, years later, I can see the universal scheme of things, a plan that inspires me to recognize just how natural the laws of the universe are. Whether conscious or unconscious, the setting of an intention will result in an exhibition of that intention. That is why it is important to prioritize your wants and needs when setting intentions.

Whenever I reflect on all of the things that I desire in life, it becomes exceptionally clear to me that peace is at the top of my list. It is fulfilling to be able to experience this extraordinary feeling of absolute peace, harmony and the inner serenity that arises from knowing my divine purpose and understanding exactly who I am. Although I am blessed to be part of this physical plane, I feel a more profound sense of gratitude because my life has awakened to a redeveloped spiritual dimension.

When you begin to fully comprehend the power of intention, you will feel comfortable embracing the truth that you are the cause of every effect in you life. Once you've gained this insight, you will take responsibility for your actions and be accountable to yourself before completing an action. Envision living with the assurance that you can have whatever you want—all you have to do is set your intention on achieving it, and it's yours! Imagine knowing this startling truth! If you want to make your wants your accomplishments, visualize embracing it.

Clearly, your intention is the most profound and intense part of your subconscious belief system. I strongly feel that people have the power to outwardly manifest their deepest intentions. As an example, I will use a rather common incident that many can relate to. Picture yourself in a restaurant. The waiter approaches and asks for your order. You browse the menu and respond, "I'll have a grilled sea bass." You clearly spoke your wishes to the server, who appears to have understood. However, twenty minutes later, you're served a steak. Frustrated, you hold the waiter responsible, accusing him of being distracted or negligent in doing his job correctly.

Maybe you should rethink your finger-pointing conclusion. Perhaps it's unfair to attribute guilt when in fact, he is not at fault. Actually, the blame lies elsewhere, because even though you specifically requested fish, in your subconscious, you really wanted the meat. You could return the mistaken order, but chances are you'll be served the steak a second time.

"I ordered sea bass." You can repeat it again and again, but in your deepest level of consciousness, the meat wins out!

Perhaps for health or dietary reasons, you contradicted your intention when the waiter appeared. You settled for the fish, really desiring the steak! But the power of your mind took control and manifested itself in the choice you made in your subconscious: *voila*—the steak!

The mind's power holds influence even in simpler situations. Your energy focuses where your intention centers it. I have experienced this even while going about completing my daily chores. When I drive to an appointment, I always visualize available parking spaces in the vicinity of where I'm headed. If I enter a parking lot and keep repeating to myself, "Oh, there are so many cars out here—there will never be a spot for me. It's so crowded today. I'll probably have to park at least a mile away and walk to where I'm going," my negative thinking will manifest itself and I won't find a convenient place. In other words, with the force of my thoughts, I bring my fear into orbit. It had nothing to do with what I wanted and all to do with what I willed, consciously or otherwise.

On the other hand, I always drive through the lot setting as my intention the availability of a space for me. I visualize it and I create it with my intention. My thoughts center on, "This is going to be quick and easy. There's always a spot for me. I'm just going to pull right in." I never have a problem parking my car.

Simple things, such as manifesting a parking space in a congested shopping center, must be considered first in order to awaken your conscious mind to the accuracy and precision of this law. When I speak about this parking spot manifestation, resulting from the setting of my intention, people will often respond, "Tonja, that could be just a coincidence or a streak of good luck. Give me a more significant or life-changing experience to prove your point with intention manifestation!"

When confronted by doubters, I say, "Listen, if you're asking for more evidence, it's apparent you don't understand the parking place incident. I suggest you explore the world of intentions by setting your own. Try it and experience your own phenomenal miracle. Awaken to the power of your mind. This personal awakening will demonstrate how your mind and your ability to focus join forces to create whatever you want."

The key is to focus on what you want and set it out into the universe, creating a source of vital energy that encircles you. And as a result, you will receive a wide spectrum of opportunities that differ from and far surpass your goals.

For instance, a goal may be, "I'm going to undertake a new business venture with Company XYZ." An intention, on the other hand would say, "I'm going to create new business opportunities that will serve me and my highest and best good." As a result, what comes to me are several prospects giving me the chance to create new opportunities, together with the universe. I'm open to the flow of this energy and accordingly, the universe is granting my deepest desire. In my mind, I had this desire as an exclusive outcome. I relied on this intention instead of calling into focus a "faking it" mindset.

You can engage yourself in a positive dialogue to reinforce your wishes; however, the content of your words has to be aligned with your desire. There is a quote often used by motivational speakers: "Fake it 'til you make it." The validity of this theory can be debated because if you fake it with words

that are not directly linked to your desire, you're not imbed-
ding it in your belief system. Consequently, you will not have
a chance to create that all-determining intentional power,
which is responsible for a successful outcome.

You can say whatever you want and pretend to be
whomever you wish, but if you don't have a sincere desire to
change, you'll just be a non-contracted actor playing a role.
Many people have approached me after my seminars and
said, "Tonja, I want to change and I want to be a multi-millionaire, but I'm not willing to do what it takes." It's not difficult to conclude that since they are not willing to do what
it takes, they are not going to get what they want. It's as simple as that.

This brings to mind another common incident that illustrates the power of change. Many of us have known people,
maybe friends or relatives, who repeatedly break up with
their spouses or partners and instinctively call to thrash the
"culprits" to the ground. They continually dig up every negative trait and rehash every failing they can drag from their
memory and spread it around. Once the temper subsides and
the stream of slander has dried out, the couple in question
reconciles. Your friend or relative has forgiven and taken back
the spurned mate. At their house, it's a candlelight supper
and chilled champagne—all is forgotten. However, for you
and everyone else in the direct line of fire, it's not washed
away with a goblet of bubbly. The slanderous, mud-flinging
onslaught remains vivid, making it difficult for you to forgive
and forget the subject of their outrage.

The friend or relative who continually falls into that pattern of behavior is choosing not to do anything different,

because they want to keep having the same derogatory conversation! Apparently, this outburst of negative energy gives them something they seek. Even if it has absolutely no bearing on what they actually say they want, it's what they want deep inside, in their subconscious.

Some people aspire to playing the victim role full-time, whereas others want to live their lives as insignificant individuals. They plant these intentions in their unconscious minds and manifest circumstances that actually keep them feeling victimized or unimportant. These people choose differently. Choice seems difficult, but as I said in Chapter 1, it's just a split-second action. I like to repeat an idea that Norman Vincent Peale expressed: "Change your thoughts and you change your world." In my opinion, those eight words are a powerful, life-altering bit of advice to follow, regardless of the initial difficulty.

I have discovered that many people tell me they start to feel uneasy when they make changes. Perhaps trading the familiar for the unfamiliar brings a fear of the unknown. It is true that change often brings discomfort. But what people fail to recognize is that the edgy, uncomfortable feeling is actually the *right thing*. I always say, "When it feels wrong, it's probably right!" It may sound somewhat ironic, but if you think about it a moment you will see the point. If you always do what feels right, why are you looking to do something different? I believe that wrong is almost right when you're considering change. You're not repeating the same behavioral patterns and redesigning the same unproductive blueprints. However, you have to be honest with yourself and realistic about your changes.

You cannot set a false intention. If you say you want to be a millionaire but deep down, you have a dreaded fear of responsibility, you lack the motivation to make a commitment to work hard diligently, and your subconscious is filled with ingrained beliefs that your life will never improve, then you will not manifest the life of a millionaire because you continue to challenge your intention.

Change takes charge when you begin to get rid of these contradictory thought patterns. This conflicting way of thinking serves only to hold you back and must be altered by consciously reprogramming your mind and revisiting the choice to design the life that you choose. I like to compare it to spring cleaning—you throw out all the stuff you've been keeping around for no good reason. By relinquishing the things that no longer serve you, a wider space will open up, allowing entry of the things that will serve you now.

Another important factor to consider when setting intentions is the time element. You can only set an intention for NOW, because there is no yesterday or tomorrow. When people tell me that there really is a yesterday, I tell them to bring it to me—"Prove it," I say. "Show it to me!" Obviously, they can't comply with my request, because yesterday really doesn't exist in this moment. It is not a living component of the NOW, just like tomorrow. We have neither the assurance nor a guarantee it will be there, because when we get to where we think the future is, it will be today, a part of the NOW. This is why I continue to emphasize that intentions are for the NOW. In essence, all we have is NOW, that is why it is so imperative that you begin to decide what you want NOW and move towards it intentionally—NOW!

Explore your intentions and ask yourself to define your objectives. What exactly do you want to do or accomplish? If you're over six feet tall, don't set an intention to become a Triple Crown-winning jockey and if you have a staid personality, don't aspire to making millions as a Seinfeld stand in! Outrageous intentions will only result in a waste of energy that could have been applied to achieving a realistic accomplishment. Once you identify what you want and are able to pinpoint the why behind your thought, you will be better equipped to choose the right course of action.

Your dreams, desires and intentions are personal—they belong to you exclusively. But having a support system of strategic alliances is an important factor in the success equation. If you do your homework diligently, you will be qualified to establish when and with whom you can discuss your intentions. Choose people who are trustworthy and willing to give you positive feedback that can actually be an asset in achieving your intentions. Locate your comfort zone and be willing to accept yourself as a person. Be self-confident about your decision-making capabilities, make your own judgment calls and step up to your own options, regardless of the opinions, criticisms, advice and action of others.

The casual millionaire is an enlightened master who searches for his or her own higher self-truth in every circumstance and condition of life. These successful individuals make every effort to serve the planet, aware that they are just one small part of a huge, cosmic force. They understand that whatever intentions they set regarding the fate or well-being of others will in effect return to them. Grasping this idea, the casual millionaire will strive to live in harmony with the

Divine Power, putting people before profit and God before the ego-dominated will of the "me and I."

I believe that when you give freely of your time, talents and treasures without expectations of a reciprocal receiving experience, you are truly giving for the sake of being a contributor to someone else.

In my *Millionaire Mindset* audio CDs, I relate an incident involving a man named Warren. It mentions an experience I had one day while rushing to a studio recording. While driving, I realized I had a flat tire. My quick thinking made me pull into the nearest gas station to see if I could get some assistance. Unfortunately, it didn't have a service station—instead, it had Warren!

Warren was dressed in tattered clothing and gave me the impression he had not enjoyed a shower in months. He approached my car, pointed to my flat tire and said, "It looks like your tire's down and you could use some help." I responded affirmatively. He asked me to open the trunk so he could get out the spare donut, the jack and the necessary tools. I was amazed to see how he took control of the situation! I was in a hurry and rather anxious to get to my destination. Although Warren picked up on my nervousness, it didn't seem to faze him. He told me step by step what he was doing. He just kept talking and talking and changing the tire at the same time. He never paused a moment until his work was completed.

Warren proceeded to tell me what I needed to resolve the issue of flat tires. I can still hear his words, recommending a can of Fix-a-Flat. "This is great stuff," he said, "and you can repair the tire without having to change it."

No longer nervous, I became intrigued with this kind man. When I looked into his blue eyes, I noticed how genuinely willing he was to assist me—no strings attached! When he finished, I said, "I'm sorry, Warren, I can't offer you recompense, because I don't have any money with me."

He smiled and replied, "No need for money—your 'thank you' is enough!"

As I drove away, he added, "I'm always here if you need anything." I asked him if he worked at the station and he said, "No, the people just let me use the restroom and hang out!"

I knew I would return to leave a little something for Warren because he sure left a huge something with me. He gave of himself so easily, effortlessly and without any expectation. I will never forget Warren and will cherish the Warrens of the world.

This brings to mind another incident I like to use in discussing the idea of giving back. A short while ago, a man approached me after a talk I was giving and debated me on the philosophy of giving to receive. He was upset with his church's appeal for financial assistance: "Tonja, I'm not participating in the tithing at my church this year. Instead, I will invest the money and make a larger commitment next year." I told him I disagreed with his intention and let it rest. The following year, I discovered that all his investments had soured. It was clear in my mind that his reluctance to give created a barrier, obstructing his ability to receive. As St. Francis of Assisi said, "For it is in giving that we receive!"

5

Pursuing Your Passions

If you're not passionate about what you're doing, quit! Chances are that whatever you're involved in, your performance is far less than spectacular. And those around you will notice that you're just not giving the best of yourself. In addition, the energy consumed completing a non-passionate task restricts you from pursuing something that you are passionate about. Instead, do what you enjoy doing and love what you do. Better still, make what you do something you love. Martha Stewart built an empire and characterized her phenomenal success in a short but to-the-point quote: "All the things I love is what my business is all about!"

Most people operate out of fear. They lock themselves in go-nowhere jobs because they're afraid of relinquishing the security blanket woven from knowing their bills will get paid.

Fear is a strong motivator, albeit a negative one. This is evidenced in the reality that people will walk further to steer clear of pain than to gain pleasure.

Throughout the years, I have observed many people who stubbornly persist in unsatisfactory jobs because they are too scared to explore other options. They feel a certain level of comfort with the familiar—if nothing else, it's a promise of security. Some individuals don't thrive on change. They're neither adventurous nor enterprising by nature, but prefer to remain with their feet solidly planted in one place because they know what they are dealing with, how to handle the situation at hand and just what to expect. In their mindset, a fear of the unknown is so paralyzing, they choose to live in the misery they are able to manage rather than relinquish the familiar to follow a new opportunity. This choice prohibits them from heading into unsheltered territory and limits their possibility to eventually find a source of enlightenment that would illuminate their life.

In my presentations, I encourage people to find what motivates them. I persuade them to look for something they are passionate about and explore how they can incorporate it into their lives for financial gain. Truly, I cannot think of any activity chosen out of love that doesn't have the potential to earn money. I'm so convinced of my belief that I'd actually challenge someone to jump up and contest me by saying, "Tonja, I love to sleep, but it won't put food on the table!" I'm ready to respond that researchers in sleep clinics pay individuals to test sleep patterns and identify the symptoms of the various disturbances leading to restlessness. It proves my theory is ironclad!

Being passionate about your wants and aspirations, and letting self-confidence as opposed to fear be your guiding light, will direct you towards positive outcomes. Start by removing your focus from the accumulation of dollars and put it on the passion. When you center on the enthusiasm and excitement associated with what you're doing, the money will flow incessantly. It's unstoppable!

This calls to mind an interesting incident that illustrates my point. Not long ago, I hired a woman to work in my office. A former school nurse for over two decades, she fell in love with the world of real estate investing and wanted to leave her job and pursue her passion. Following one of my seminars, she approached me, somewhat petrified because I had mentioned she could dabble in real estate on a part-time basis. "Tonja," she said, "I realize I could do this part time, but I love it. I want to be involved full-time! This is all I want to do. I would like to research and preview properties. I want to study for my broker's license, learn about building codes and become familiar with the MLS."

This courageous woman acted on her intentions, took a huge leap of faith and left her job even before she had the security of an income from her real estate option. Following a financially "dry" year, she became involved in a condo conversion project and brought in over $2,000,000. The moral of the story is that doing what she was passionate about presented an opportunity for her to more than quadruple her income. She followed the beat of her own drummer, let her zest for real estate be her catalyst and enjoyed a profitable outcome. Making the change, she let go of what was holding her back—the nursing job—and moved forward, undaunted by a fear of the unknown. After a twenty-year, so-so career, she set a different intention that was manifested in her success. Using the power of her mind, she rewrote the script that redesigned her life.

I'm from a Midwest, beach-challenged territory, and I remember my first impression of California. Driving along the coast, I spotted what appeared to be endless displays of people savoring the sun and surf while having fun relaxing. At that time, I remarked to myself, "All these sunbathers seem so carefree—they certainly know how to enjoy life." However, idyllic as it seemed, in reality, those beach mongers were only enjoying life from one limited perspective—physical relaxation and a brief moment of pleasure. In reality, they could not truly enjoy life if they were not where they desired to be financially. Therefore, their feelings of contentment were just linked to a specific momentum. On one hand, there was a rush of well-being, but on the other, it was fleeting and not an integral part of their lifestyle.

I tell people who attend my seminars that in order to live a balanced life, it is necessary to create a harmonious relationship between the two perspectives. And the key to building this equilibrium rests in motivation, inspiration and passion. Your passion inspires and inspiration, in turn, motivates! However, the energy for movement and change originates in the passion. It's the life force of success.

Whenever I give a presentation on the determining factor of passion, I always imagine people either approaching me or raising their hands to ask me, "But Tonja, that sounds fine and great, but how do you find what you're passionate about?" Puzzling as it may be to understand, it's true—some people are clueless about what they love doing. This could be attributed to the fact that perhaps it's been years since anyone asked them about what fires them up or maybe they stopped asking themselves. As a result, they find themselves incessantly riding on the carousel of a daily routine that involves sliding out of bed and trotting off to work. They're living a programmed existence, doing what they have to do, not what they like to do. This uncreative philosophy of compromise, imbedded in their subconscious, manifests itself in frustration and fruitless outcomes.

On the other hand, if their mindset focused on a "do what you love to do and make what you do something you love" intention, they would be able to alter and re-channel their entire energy sources to attract a different set of circumstances and scenarios. New opportunities would spring, which would open the door to meeting diverse people. It's about renovating your attitude to remodel your outcome so that your income appreciates!

Let's get back to the question I sometimes imagine people will ask: "How do I discover where my passions lie?" My take on this is that you can get passionate about just loving what you do. It's easy, if you just tell yourself, "This is not the greatest job in the world but I love the fact that I am the person who is actually doing it. I love that I come to work every morning. I'm thrilled to be the person who lights up this office. I love that I get to show people things in a way that no one else has thought of or carried out before. I find being able to use my abilities and talents for profit to be a gratifying return on the investment of my time and energy."

This mental exercise goes back to the idea that being

good at everything you do unlocks doors and presents opportunities. Therefore, if you decide to be passionate about what you do every day, just because you're doing it, you will have taken the first step towards changing your life. Consider the things you do without obligation, command or instruction—those activities and tasks that occupy a space in your leisure hours. In what circumstances, if at all, do you step up to bat when no one asks or expects you to? What initiatives do you take? What are you willing to do for your own serenity? It's your free time—and how do you fill it?

Most people will respond, "Well, since I really don't have any off-time, I can't answer the question!" I'm always skeptical about this quick to toss into the wind response and my instinctive come-back is: "You have to find your passion. To start, get rid of the radio; turn off the TV and cell phone; put down the senseless tabloids or glossy magazines that consume your attention; postpone the temptation to call a friend and gossip. Instead, invite yourself for an afternoon or evening alone. Sit down and learn to experience yourself. Enjoy your own company in a quiet place where distractions won't interrupt your dialogue with the self. If you use those moments of silence to explore different options, you will discover what you're passionate about. The first couple of times may be white elephants. Perhaps you'll feel uncomfortable with the silence and bored by the whole idea of spending time with yourself."

The truth is that the very things obstructing this process are in fact the toys of a modern and highly technological society. And oddly enough, you can't do without them. These radios, TVs and computers stop you from thinking. It's amazing how many people don't think. I'm often asked the most ridiculous questions, and although I've always said no question is stupid, many are ludicrous. The sad part is that these preposterous inquiries are spun out of laziness. People don't even give themselves a chance to answer their own question. They throw it out for someone else to answer because they're so accustomed to pushing things off on others. From morning until evening, someone tells them what to do, who to talk to and where to go. It becomes a habit not to think. Maybe Henry Ford was making a good point when he said, "Thinking is hard work, which is why so few people do it!" My spin on thinking is that if you want to be successful, you have to be able to think on your own—and if you're thinking about what you're passionate about, you will like your thoughts. When you like your thoughts, it is easy to turn them into profitable actions. That is how success is born.

If the non-thinkers would have paused a moment, they would have realized they could have used their own resources to suction out their own brainpower and answer their own question. But in today's society, we are all geared towards the "just ask someone else" mechanism. It's quick and it's easy. However, effortless as it may be, it comes with no guarantee that the answer we receive from others is the correct one. This "uncomplicated way out" for a lot of people equates to basing their career choice on the suggestions, opinions and advice someone else imparted. It's an undemanding approach that requires neither energy nor responsibility. Well, one thing is certain—without an investment, there can be no profit!

Many times, I've heard someone say, "Okay, I'll take the

job in the dental office because *you* work there and there's an opening. That's a real lifesaver. Now, I don't have to read the classifieds any more!" What an unproductive mindset. Just because one person's passion may be working in a dental office doesn't mean it's exhilarating for another. This is a prime example of followers who travel with the flow, never taking the lead in their own lives. They go where they're "sent" to go, like puppets on a string in the hand of an "architect" who knows absolutely nothing about the floor plan of their passions. Consequently, people who don't take the initiative to become acquainted with themselves make landfall in places in which they have no business being. This is a recipe for unhappiness and failure.

But if you persist with the exercise to uncover your own passions, you will be amazed by the surplus of options that will materialize before you. Life has a way of moving you forward, helping you determine what you're meant to do and more importantly, leading you to realize what you're truly passionate about. It's an *epiphanous* event; it happens and you're enlightened!

I have always been passionate about teaching. I remember how even as a young child, I would gather my friends around and find things to teach them. My specialties were showing them how to ride a bike or how to play baseball. Later on, when in the military, I was drawn towards a career as a training instructor because it satisfied my desire to show others how to do something I already knew. I was the same age as the recruits, yet I was teaching them how to exist in the military, how to get the most out of basic training and the correct way to march. Eventually, I moved into the academic sphere, teaching them different subjects that were of use to advance their careers.

I was also passionate about trying to simplify a complex scenario. I learned a long time ago that most individuals have the reading skills suitable for a seventh-grade level. Based on this discovery, I'm always conscious about and take extra precautions to speak and instruct according to that standard, because I want people to "get it" and to be able to adapt my ideas to make the positive changes in their lives that will produce prosperity. Relaying information and helping people achieve their objectives is another "branch" of my passion.

I believe this is linked to my mom, who was my muse, motivating and encouraging me. I strongly feel her power to inspire was attributed to the fact that she neither satisfied her desires nor had a chance to live out her own passions. Although she did have a blazing fervor for raising the children, deep down, I believe there were many unrealized realms she never really got a chance to explore. However, through me, she emphasized her own ungratified feelings. It was clear to me she wanted my life to be different and certainly more stimulating. Even today, I can still hear her words: "Tonja, do something you love, do something you really want to do." In the end, she was responsible for my formative experiences in the military, which eventually led to my final decision to leave after I realized I wanted to set my intention on making a lot of money.

John D. Rockefeller believed, "The road to happiness lies in two simple principles: find what interests you and that you can do well, and put your whole soul into it—every bit of energy and ambition and natural ability you have!"

This shines a light on the mindset of a successful businessman and philanthropist and demonstrates how doing what you love and letting your passion work brings about the prosperity you desire.

Making money was always a passion of mine and I knew from early on that whatever I would choose to do would give me the wealth I wanted. Sometimes, people ask, "Tonja, what does passion have to do with becoming the casual millionaire?"

My response is one and the same whenever I'm questioned: "I think passion has everything to do with becoming the casual millionaire! It's a secret that is really not a secret—a revealed hush-hush." If you stop and think about it, it's just the plain truth. You can't make money if you're not passionate about making money! Some people are afraid to say, "I'm passionate about making money," because they're intimated by the biblical passage that reads, "Money is the root of all evils." However, if they would understand the correct interpretation, they would realize, it's the *love* of money that is condemned as the root of all evils.

Being passionate about acquiring wealth does not imply worshiping money. Instead, it entails finding comfort and reassurance in pursuing it and discovering ways of putting your passion to work, for the creation of your fortune.

Just several days ago, a real estate agent attending one of my seminars stood up and said, "Tonja, I feel *guilty* if I make too much money!"

Instinctively, I replied, "Do you, really?"

"Yes," she said. "I feel so guilty. I have more money than my friends! I have more than my family!"

"Did you make too much money last year?" I responded.

"Yes," she said, almost breathless.

"How much was too much?" I asked, intrigued by her reply.

"Oh, about $40,000!" she whispered.

"Well," I said. "Do you have your check book with you?"

She looked at me with a puzzled expression. I quickly un-puzzled her look by saying, "If you take out your check book, I'll take the extra $40,000 that's riddling you with guilt!"

When she broke into laughter, I said, "Why are you laughing? You said you felt guilty, so I'm offering you a way to eliminate your guilty feelings! If the extra 40 grand is so disturbing, just give it away and you'll feel better."

"Well, no," she replied. "I don't want to do that, either!"

"Listen," I said. "If you don't want to give away what you claim is the reason for your guilt, then the truth is, you real-ly don't feel guilty at all, because if you did, you would have to get rid of the money. Apparently, you have found another way to 'clear your conscience.' So how are you doing it—what are you doing?"

"Well, Tonja," she said after taking a deep breath, "what I do is, I spend the money frivolously. I buy gifts for every-one, instead of treating myself."

"There you go," I answered. "You're getting rid of it! It's a great 'guilt buster,' but what's in it for you? Surely, you don't have what you want. First, you're making money, and then you're disposing of it. You're blowing it on other people and making them feel good because you feel so bad about having made the money. The point is, you want to make them feel good about you spending it on them!"

I focused on this during the seminar, discussing it in more detail, and concluded: "My take on this incident is that your own self-worth is at the core of this dilemma. You simply don't feel like you deserve the money—because if you think you're unworthy, you'll find ways to channel it away from you."

Another facet of passion is having the self-confidence to accept and feel comfortable with what you deserve. Understanding your passion, knowing what you love to do and being reassured that every dime you receive from doing what you're good at and like doing is well merited. Living your life with passion makes you eligible to receive the wealth you earn.

One of the things I like to incorporate in my seminar is a visualization exercise. I encourage people to personally experience their lives exactly as they are today, but two decades later—as if nothing changed except for the year. They've made no changes, no life-altering decisions and no progress. Everything is frozen in time, except that they are twenty years older! Then, I ask them to express their feelings. The "experiment" ends with most of the people feeling disillusioned, ungratified and unfilled—in other words, awful and despondent. It's an unbearable vision!

After the "moment of truth" reaction, I tell them to visualize their lives as ideal. I encourage them to imagine they have achieved all their objectives, have succeeded in obtaining everything they ever wanted and were where they always dreamed to be. I designed a scenario in which each individual had a life filled with whatever he or she wished. They had it all—enormous wealth, wonderful relationships and spiritual harmony.

Following the misery of their initial downcast panorama, I created an optimistic picture of a brilliant future. It was pain pitted against pleasure—anger, distress and inner turbulence versus joy, self-fulfillment and peace of mind. I demonstrated how if they kept themselves imprisoned in an uneventful life, they would continue to have what they have now and grow only in their misery as they grew old!

The reactions to my exercise were dramatic! People cried out in anguish, became physically ill and doubled over in agony, clutching their stomachs. It was a release of the suffering attached to living a life of waste. In fact, the most horrifying aspect of the human condition is the terror of stagnation. People thrive on change, change is synonymous with growth and growth is the continuation of life.

Passion is the life force that drives you toward something; think about MADD (Mothers Against Drunk Driving), started by a mother who lost a child to an inconsiderate drunk driver. This woman had a cause she was passionate about and a situation that motivated her to action.

In my life, passion is a priority. I awaken every morning loving life and the activities I'm involved in. I love the people in my life and I love to celebrate life as if I'm seeing it for the first time through the eyes of a small, innocent child. It's an awesome experience.

With passion, all things are possible—with passion, everything is easy. However, when passion withers, relationships collapse, business becomes a burden and life takes on the frightening hollowness of nothingness. Keeping passion alive requires a loyal, full-time commitment, but it's well worth the effort, since in essence it's the very "pulse" of life.

Without it, man becomes disconnected from the Divine Power—this being the case, a death of the spirit will rule!

In my life, I've observed the diverse cycles of my own relationships. I always desire to be on that euphoric high of the first date. I love the initial falling in love scenario where neither they nor I could do any wrong—we were perfect! Until the bubble of illusion burst and suddenly, I noticed the one tiny, microscopic flaw that magnified in my mind and became the most horrible character trait a person could have. Thus ended the relationship.

Once again, I began my search for that special feeling of something new, better or excitingly different. I remember how shocked I was when I realized that there wasn't anything or anyone that could be more fulfilling, better or different, until I became the person I wanted to date and be around: that better woman, that different woman! Hmmm…I had reached an amazing conclusion! I had to be all that I wanted so that I would not *want* for anything. Nobody and nothing would complete or satisfy me, because I myself would be whole, perfect and complete. Then, I had an awakening! I noticed that the more I liked myself, the more I knew who I was and what I wanted, the more attractive I became to others in personal and professional relationships.

I had a life-altering, born again experience! I shed my old skin and way of thinking and awakened to a new idea that encompassed how I could change my life and live my days with real, burning passion. I no longer looked to another person to enrich my life with what I thought was lacking because I decided I had the power and the possibility to enhance my own life. Neediness can be a relationship buster if we allow it to take over our lives. A productive life change is synonymous with needing nothing and expecting nothing. And as a result of this growth experience, you gain everything!

When I discuss relationships in my seminars, people often approach me at the end and ask, "Tonja, what do relationships have in common with the passion of a casual millionaire?"

"Well," I respond, "becoming wildly wealthy is about passion. Living is about passion! And life is filled with all types of relationships, not just romantic. The objective is to become that very person you yourself can fall in love with. Then, sit back and watch as the world falls in love with you!

Evaluate what you love in other people. You will notice that in your love and adoration, you will find traits you hold in common. Likewise, you will also find traits you can relate to in the disturbing habits and faults of others. Use what you gather to redesign your life and move forward to live your intentions.

Remember, to keep passions alive, you must commit to letting them thrive in your life. Work towards creating it. No doubt, there will be ups and downs. But if you put it all on the scale, you will be able to see if the good is worth the bad or if in effect, you have created an intolerable imbalance.

Human beings yearn for expansion and development. We are born to grow and move forward and become more in tune with the Divine Power, from which we all originated. Anything that trumps that process of opening out and spreading our wings to explore and conquer new horizons suffocates our spirituality and life force. This is why pursuing your passions is an important commitment. As Alfred Lord Tennyson so nobly wrote, "The happiness of a man in this life does not consist in the absence but in the mastery of his passions."

6

Loading the Millionaire Mindset

How you think governs how you act and how you act determines the nature of your outcomes. As previously stated, the mind is the mechanism that sets you in movement. If you're not moving fast enough, maybe it's time to reprogram your thoughts—upgrade what is potentially lucrative and delete the "stinking thinking" program that is obstructing your path.

To better understand the workings of the millionaire mindset, I like to compare and contrast it to the average person's way of thinking, which I associate with the poor mindset. This latter state of thinking walks hand in hand with a "woe is me" attitude that falls back on the self-appointed poor victim status. These eternal chastisers always look to cast blame elsewhere for their failings. Their reasoning for not achieving objectives is based on the faults and irresponsibility of other individuals. This finger-pointing definition of why they accomplish little is actually the motivation behind their zero success quotients. It's always someone else's fault when things don't quite turn out right—never theirs. George Washington Carver cleverly summoned it up when he said, "Ninety-nine percent of the failures come from people who have a habit of making excuses!"

I have helped many low-income families with zero available funds find suitable housing. Whenever I put an opportunity on the table, they accept it animatedly and are grateful the day they move in. However, somewhere along the way, responsibility and accountability fall to the wayside! They don't maintain their part of the agreement.

Not long ago, I met a family in financial difficulty. The husband was a teacher at a local school and his wife held an administrative post in the same institution. Together with their two children, the couple was living as guests of the wife's sister and was eager to get their own place.

One day, the sister approached me. "Tonja," she said quite anxiously, "my sister, brother-in-law and their kids are driving me nuts. I have to get them out of my house and into a place of their own!"

I interviewed the couple and learned that their combined income was just bordering on $120,000 in the California market. The husband informed me he had recently received a promotion to teach at the college level if he pursued a master's degree. He had agreed and was *en route* to the east coast to complete the course.

"Tonja," he said, "things are tight right now. I don't have the money to pay for this, so I'll be studying and living at the university for a couple of years while my wife and kids remain here in California. But my primary objective is to get a house for my family to live in while I'm gone. I'd be so grateful if someone could offer me some assistance."

"Well" I said, "I happen to have a house available that I can sell you on this day next year, if you make all your payments on time. I'll reduce the rent and let you lease it for $1,000 under the current market value. If you meet your monthly rental payments, I'll help you qualify to buy this property and I will give you a hand with your mortgage payments by taking on a partnership with you in that transaction for the next fifteen years. You will have the home you want and with my foundation, I'll lighten your financial obligation by taking on $1,000 of your mortgage responsibility."

"That's fabulous," he said. Soon after, we put the transaction in motion and the family moved into the house.

Less than a week later, I received a call from the husband, who breathlessly recited a list of grievances, cataloging everything that was less than perfect in the house. The truth is that the lease agreement specifically stated it was their responsibility as tenants to take care of all the repairs, since they were in occupancy and the house would become their property in a year. It was a nice piece of property, certainly not dilapidated or neglected.

One afternoon, he phoned me, complaining that the sprinklers were malfunctioning and the lawn was turning brown. I advised him to use the hose until I could call someone to repair the watering system. He refused to hand-water and insisted I replace the sprinklers. His refusal to pick up the hose resulted in a dried out, burnt lawn.

It didn't end with the sprinklers. He phoned me in continuation with the most nonsensical complaints, like reporting a hairline crack in the bathroom, in an area where the caulking had peeled from the wall. In response, I reminded him, "Listen, Wesley, our agreement specified that you would assume responsibility for minor flaws and issues that didn't require major repairs. For you to phone every time something minor occurs is ridiculous. You're going to be the owner of this property and when that occurs, you cannot come to me with every failing, small or otherwise."

One month later, he defaulted on the rental payment. I phoned him to inquire why he was negligent. "Tonja," he responded, "I'm not going to send you the check this month until my bathroom gets caulked!"

I interrupted my schedule, put my appointments on hold and went over to the house. "Wesley," I said. "Let me explain something to you. I'm going to serve you with what is known as a three-day notice to pay your rent!"

I asked him to show me the peeled caulking that was at the root of his contention. We walked over to the bathroom and he pointed towards the wall in question. I noticed the crack was hardly visible. I served him the notice and simultaneously, he deposited the rental check in my hand. "Wesley," I said, "I hope this incident will not be repeated. It's disturbing and makes me feel like I'm pulling back on my commitment to help you. Your behavior is crazy! I thought you were heading to the east coast for your master's. Why aren't you following your initial plan?"

"Well," he responded, "actually, I had some medical problems with my knee. I had to have surgery and complete weeks of therapy afterwards—and there were other things in between."

"So when did all this come up?" I asked, realizing he had been living in the house just one month!

"Oh, well, just recently," he blurted. "It happened all of a sudden! Kind of caught me off guard and upset my plans!"

"No, Wesley," I said. "This problem probably surfaced before you moved into the house. You just didn't say anything!" In reality, this was quite a different scenario from the original. He was unemployed, with endless time to spare, utilizing it to barrage me with phone calls to "bring to my attention" the most trivial things.

Eventually, his wife phoned me and asked if I could lay out some payment arrangements that would be agreeable for everyone. She wanted to take into consideration when her checks arrived and she would be able to send a check. I agreed. Well, even today, I'm still dealing with him on a weekly basis. Wesley calls with the most ridiculous complaints and idiotic grievances. One day he phoned, disturbed because a fire truck drove through his neighborhood at two in the morning! I don't know how, when or why, but in some mystifying way, this was my fault, and no one else was to blame. I had the exclusive on that guilt!

I bring this incident to light and sometimes discuss it at my seminars because it demonstrates the influence of mindset on a given outcome. People say they want to help themselves and their families but build the blocks that obstruct their own paths. Their thinking hinges on somebody trying to take something away from them; someone is planning to make a fool out of them; somebody is trying to hurt them— someone is always doing something to them. In addition to the faulty thinking, they are gratitude-challenged individuals who expect if not down outright demand to get what they want.

Many times, I find that some lower-income people live on outrageous expectations. They feel as if they are victims, slighted in the grand scheme of things, and consequently, they believe the world owes them big time. Feeling as if they have been unjustly wronged, it's the duty of others to make amends. This example clearly illustrates the substance of the poor mindset.

Thomas Edison said, "Many of life's failures are people who did not realize how close they were to success when they gave up." It's about reforming your mindset to bring in the thoughts that will lead you to follow through on your intentions. Often, faulty thinking can be either a roadblock or a shackle, holding you in check.

Exploring the mindset is an interesting exercise, especially when you observe wealthy and poor people. The differences are phenomenal. In essence, the mindset is the "parent" of the multi-millionaire or the destitute soul.

This is the mantra of success: "I'm capable; it's easy; I'm going to; I am doing; I can and I will. I take responsibility; I'm fully accountable; I'll figure it out; I'll see how to work it out; I'll find the perfect solution; I'll create win-win scenarios. I'll study and research it and let's ban together and pool our resources." This is the millionaire mindset. It helps you create the income you deserve.

On the flip side, the other mindset destroys you and demolishes everything in your path that is coming to help you. There isn't a sane person alive who dreams about being in the company of a victim! Nobody wants to spend their energy offering assistance to an individual who they feel will be neither appreciative nor grateful. And I truly doubt anyone enjoys receiving a slap in the face when he or she reaches out to give a hand. I see this over and over again as I watch people in my own company trying to employ others who either misrepresent themselves or lie outright.

Personally, I've experienced it in my foundation. I remember one incident in particular. An impoverished family needed a truck to be able to get their hauling business rolling. It was provided for them on the condition that they would present themselves for work on time. In exchange for the vehicle, this was the only commitment I expected. When the truck was delivered, the gentleman did not show up for work—not the following day, not a week later, but the very *same* day he received delivery!

I phoned him and said, "Morgan, where are you? You're supposed to be at work!"

"Oh, Tonja," he lied, "I had something going on that I had to take care of and couldn't get to work. I'm still trying to get things done."

I was seated just four houses down the street from his and, although he did not know, I was able to see everything that was happening—or in this case, not happening.

"Morgan," I said, "I can see you! You're not doing what you just told me you were doing!"

"Well, where are you?" he grunted.

"I'm right here down the street," I said. "Come over and see for yourself."

The truck was repossessed because Morgan failed to maintain his end of the deal. By defaulting on his commitment, he forfeited a potentially good opportunity.

The moral to this incident is that people cannot help you if you don't have the right mindset for success. Morgan's mindset should have focused on keeping his commitment, regardless of unpredictable circumstances. He should have told himself, "I made a commitment to show up for work and no matter what, no matter how difficult it is to get up in the morning, I'm sticking with it." If you're committed to maintaining your part of an agreement, you should have your mindset programmed to tell you, "I'm going to do it; I'm going to get up and I'll show up."

If you choose not to show up, change the program to, "I'm going to get out of bed, stand up and make a phone call to say, 'I choose not to show up.'"

Wealthy individuals don't depend on absurd excuses like the ridiculous calls I sometimes receive from my administrative staff, frantically blaming the congested Los Angeles highway for their repeated tardiness. "Oh, the traffic! Oh, the traffic!" is supposed to exonerate all fault. Typically, I'll say; "Well, how long have you lived in California?" Most of the time the response will be, "I've lived here my whole life!" In response, I'll inquire if today's traffic is worse than yesterday's.

The point is, you plan ahead for both predictable and unforeseen circumstances. In a high traffic situation, you get up early and allow an extra half hour, knowing the road will be congested during the morning rush hour. The other day, a girl in my office, whom I had just hired, came running in almost thirty minutes late. "I'm so sorry, I'm so sorry," she blurted out breathlessly. "I know that I'm late and I promised you I'd always be on time but the traffic was awful."

I took one look at her disheveled, bed-head hair and said, "And of course, you just woke up!"

"Well, yeah," she murmured.

I continued, "So, was it the traffic or your poor planning?"

Her comeback was a repeat of the "Well, the traffic was atrocious" line. It was more than evident she had silenced the alarm, rolled off the mattress twenty minutes later and made a mad dash for the car. Even if she was the sole driver on the road, she could not have reached the office on time.

When she came in for an interview, I emphasized that there was one thing that would motivate me to terminate her employment—and that involved arriving late for work.

I looked at her and said, "Listen, I'm going to give you one more chance to answer my question—was it the traffic or your poor planning?"

"Well," she said, fidgeting, "it was probably both."

"Okay," I replied. "I guess half way is better than nothing. You demonstrate some sense of responsibility and I'm always willing to accept accountability."

Her thinking was focused on a "when in trouble or on the spot, just make something up" mindset, which shares no common ground with the multi-millionaire way of thinking. The responsible person with the wealthy mindset would not make it up to get out of it. They would simply say, "This is how and why it happened and I apologize!" No excuses, ifs, ands or buts.

Look at Donald Trump as an example. He's a very straightforward man who tells it like it is, without nuances or shadings. When asked a question, you get a quick, to-the-point answer. No digressing, no beating around the bush! He has that clearly defined edge that people often mistakenly identify as a harshness of character, when in reality, he's responsible for his words and actions. He's a no-nonsense multi-millionaire.

I heard Trump in a radio interview not long ago, and the interviewer was chiding him about his "numerous bankruptcies." He criticized Donald for bankrupting his hotel in Las Vegas. The interviewer kept saying, "Well, it's true. You're really declaring the hotel bankrupt!"

Mr. Trump curtly responded, "Let me answer this. That hotel represents less than one percent of my overall net worth. I'm not even interested in talking about it!"

Frustrated, the interviewer couldn't grasp what was happening. Insistent in his way of questioning, he continued: "Let's talk about the hotel." And Mr. Trump, always in control of the situation, was determined and persistent in his retort. He fired back, "Let's talk about other things, because that is so trite and insignificant in the big picture." In reality, Mr. Trump knew that the interviewer wanted to focus on the negative, believing he had a shocking story, but what represented a negative to him was nothing worth wasting energy on for the billionaire real estate tycoon.

Another facet of the multi-millionaire mindset is big-picture thinking, which is in sharp contrast with the small-picture focus of the poor mindset. For example, if you ask people with wealthy mindsets (but not necessarily wealthy bank accounts) where they would like to go on vacation, they will name twenty or thirty options, describe the places and tell you excitedly what they read about each location. That same question asked of a poor mindset individual will result in an answer of, "Vacation! I don't have time or money to take a vacation!" The answer spills out so fast and instinctively, it appears as if they studied the script their whole lives and know the lines as soon as they hear the cue question! If you try to deprogram their mindset by asking them to think about where they might enjoy visiting, they have to really pause and think about it. Then, if encouraged further, they'll just respond with a destination spot close to home.

The wealthy mindset converts circumstances into opportunities, whereas small-picture thinking defines everything as something that has to be done. Once again, the big-picture thinkers have a wide, panoramic vision. They see it; they feel it; they fully participate in it. If you ask a wealthy mindset individual, "How do you see the next year of your life?" you will receive a vivid account with every aspect precisely detailed, down to the utmost degree.

On the other hand, the same question posed to people with poor mindsets will net a "What do you mean—what are you talking about?" response. If you persist with a "Can't you imagine it? Try to visualize it" comeback, you'll get a lackadaisical, "Hmm…Well, no, I can't see it. I guess it'll be the same as tomorrow" reply. And if you take it even further and tell them, "No, it won't be the same. Can't you imagine something different? Can't you see your life a year from now in a diverse light? Try to set it up as a motion picture playing on a screen in front of you"—the response will always be less than exalting.

When I asked a woman in my seminar to envision her life before her eyes like a film, she responded, "Oh, God, no!" What a revealing response, I thought to myself! In reality, this small-picture thinking lady felt her life would remain static. She couldn't visualize a change, was in denial and actually did not want to see herself in the future in the same role in which she was cast today.

The big-picture thinker has neither the time nor desire for denial. They confront reality, scrutinize it, pick at it and devise solutions to improve it. In contrast, the small-picture thinker escapes in a self-created pretense that reality is non-existent and lives the same life, anyway, repeating the identical experiences of the previous year.

Small-picture thinking sends negative energy into the universe. However, all is not lost. There is hope for improvement, because a mindset can evolve and change. Maybe it's time for a makeover. Learn self-motivation and gain the knowledge needed to expand your picture-thinking vision. Minds are comparable to computers. Although they have been programmed, they can be rebooted and reformatted. And best of all, you can reprogram your mind with any data you wish, as long as you truly desire it. I'm not going to tell you it's an easy process, because it takes energy and commitment. Proof of the strong effort required is evidenced in the actuality that everyone is not a multi-millionaire. If it were truly all smooth sailing, the success quotient would reach 100 percent. As Samuel Johnson said, "What is easy is seldom excellent!"

The reprogramming process is about literally exploring your desires and latching onto your passions. The following segment involves deciphering you plan of action. Your initial step should be the realization that your mind is the most powerful tool and the most prolific resource you possess on your physical being. If you don't nourish and nurture your mind, you can't take care of your body. In addition, if you can't cultivate your mind, you cannot foster or cherish anything or anyone because as I said earlier, what you think about, you bring about! And what you focus on expands! Control your mind and insert positive affirmations into your subconscious. Train yourself to believe what you say, even if at first you may be dubious. Persistence will pay a dividend and eventually, you will feel comfortable and convinced about what you're repeating.

If you walked around every day for thirty days chanting thirty times a day, "I am a multi-millionaire in the making. I'm increasing my income every second of every day. I'm feeling better and better about what I do and how much money I make. I feel competent. I feel I can make more money than I ever have before because I know I deserve it"—your life would change.

In my seminars, I challenge people to draw up a list of positive affirmations they can say every day, at least in the mornings and in the evenings. I offer encouragement, sharing my personal experience. Years ago, I read a book titled, *The Secrets of Super Selling: Programming your Subconscious Mind for Success.*

I remember that after each chapter, the author included a page of affirmations. When I finished the book, I made a commitment to read the affirmations every single morning. I paper clipped the pages at the conclusion of all ten chapters so I could view the affirmations without having to flip through the entire book.

Many times, I was tempted to bail on my commitment because I didn't have time or was just too tried. It certainly was not easy, but I was loyal to my self-pledge and went through the "programming exercise" religiously. In sticking to my commitment, I was able to see the remarkable changes that were taking place. I spoke differently, my thoughts took on another perspective and I noticed I carried myself with more self-confidence after I recited my litany. It was a powerful, life-altering process that reformatted my mindset.

Today, I continue reciting affirmations as a daily ritual. The difference is that I now create my own and don't have to resort to paper clipped pages in another person's book. I know what I want and need to say and how and when I want to say it. This is a wonderful objective to achieve. Create your own affirmations to focus on the outcome you desire in your life to cancel what you don't want. Use positive affirmations to nourish your mind: "I wake up every morning feeling money flows into my life easily and effortlessly!"

In your social and professional relationships, surround yourself with people who will affirm you—positive people who have faith in your capabilities—people who encourage, motivate and stimulate you. In other words, fill your life with people who bring out the best in you. If you patronize individuals who belittle you or who offer only demolishing criticism, it's time to "relocate to a new neighborhood!"

If you look around and see negative people, chances are that the negativity lies in you. There is a story about a gentleman on a journey who walks from town to town. In the first town, he loves the people he encounters. He finds them exhilarating and friendly and their feeling about him is reciprocal. When he visits the second town, he is approached by a gentleman who says, "What are the people like in the town you just left?"

"Oh, they were fabulous," he responds, "absolutely incredible."

"That's great," the man says excitedly, "and it's good to know, because the people in the town you're heading to are not so nice."

The man continues his journey and discovers that even these people are wonderful. They greet him warmly, treat him kindly and love him. On his return trip, he meets once again the man who asked him about the people in the first town.

"I imagine you hated that last town you visited," the gentleman tells him. "I bet you hated it. I warned you they were not nice to me when I visited. And by the way, the town you told me was filled with fabulous people was just as awful! They were all so mean and nasty to me. It was an awful visit. I couldn't wait to get away!"

The moral here is that it's all in your outlook and in the manner in which you perceive things. What may be a pleasant experience for one individual may be a dreaded nightmare for another. Perception comes from within; it's personal and individual. Before I traveled, I would visit local areas and think they were absolutely fabulous. When I broadened my horizons, my outlook and viewpoint evolved and expanded and my previous opinions no longer corresponded with my new perspectives. I also noted that what was a paradise for one person was a slum for another.

Positive people are attracted to optimistic and constructive people and repelled by negative people. They sift out individuals who deplete their energy and put a distance between them. Once again, this is the difference between the multi-millionaire mindset and the small-picture thinkers. The former recognize they don't have time for unconstructive situations or individuals because they know the value of their time and resources and are not willing to allow someone to trespass on their space and drain their vital energy. These big-picture thinkers have already made a conscious decision that they want their lives to be positive, profitable and influential.

What they don't want is something that takes away from their optimistic outcome. Therefore, it is important to determine who the confident and positive people are and establish whether you're linking with them or steering clear of them. Observe individuals who have acquired what you aspire to. Single out those people who are doing what you dream to do. Surround yourself with the successful and train yourself mentally, physically and emotionally to be who and what you want to be. Choose and create your own reality. Be responsible for your personal well-being. Build a mental, emotional and physical wellness plan and commit to it! Coach your mindset to focus on working smart and being flexible, tenacious, persistent and loyal to your intentions. Program your thinking to move towards who you want, what you want and what is profitable—and away from what you don't want and what and who will hold you back from achieving.

Choices and decisions are not necessarily easy to make. You have two options—you can either drag negative influences and people around with you or you can move away from them. This latter alternative is somewhat complicated when the unproductive people are family members.

Personally, I love the mindset of the skeptics—those somewhat dubious friends who, when you rush to inform them of your plans to embark on a new journey that involves assuming the multi-millionaire mindset, talking to yourself about positive affirmations, motivating yourself and reprogramming your thoughts, will respond, "Be careful what they tell you to load in your mind. They might be brainwashing you!"

The point is that these skeptical friends may be uncomfortable with the uncertainty of what will happen once you load the multi-millionaire mindset. They fear that once you're reprogrammed, motivated and optimistic, what will you think of them? If you use your affirmations to lose weight, eat healthy, stop smoking and get physically fit, they question if perhaps they are required to meet the same expectations, fearful they will not be able to succeed. Whatever you become or choose to become is often viewed as a threat to the other people in your circle, especially if they are unwilling to take on the same challenge.

It is important to become familiar with the language patterns of both wealthy and poor mindset people. When you can distinguish the two types of communication, you will be in a better position to make conscious decisions regarding what you are willing to share with them in conversation and how much of your time you are inclined to spend in their company. However, it is not necessary to sever all connections with a hatchet chop and a "You're a negative person and I'm not subjecting myself to likes of you anymore" farewell, which is not exactly a healthy mindset. Instead, you can learn the art of limitation. Why not change a dinner appointment to a low-fat muffin and skinny latte meeting? You re-proportion your time and nobody is offended!

In order to expand your mindset, you have to sandblast your environment. Once the debris is removed, you can treat the area with things and people that will help your thoughts grow healthy and strong, enabling your mind to permeate your body with energy infusions.

Mindset development also depends on questions. Ask yourself questions—what do you want to achieve and how do you plan to accomplish your objective? Pose your inquiries in a different way. Don't use the same old words you've been saying for decades. Scramble the lyrics on the CD in your head. Employing new words will lead to receiving new answers. When you awaken tomorrow morning, don't throw out the same question: "How am I going to get through the day?" Ask yourself instead, "What am I going to do today to get me one step closer to my objective?"

I often ask myself, "What do I need to do next? What's the next thing I should do to get me just one step closer to my intention? If I were to discover something different, what haven't I considered yet? What am I not doing? What should I do today that I didn't do yesterday or a week ago? Where I am missing a piece of the puzzle? What am I not focusing on? What will make my life different? What will make my life more joyful and fulfilling today? How can I intensify my passions? How can I get more inspired?"

You won't get an answer to your queries, but as you continue to ask the questions, your brain will start to switch gears and move at a faster pace to find the responses. You will discover that the things you do will bring you results. The mind is a phenomenal tool and the amount of information it can store is inestimable. Most people don't even make a dent in their supply of brainpower. Human potential is fabulous, but it's exhausted if not used. I always tell people that what you *can* do and what you *will* do are worlds apart.

Years ago, I met a young, twenty-two-year–old gentleman and recognized he had enormous potential as a Real Estate Agent. He was already making $100,000 a year, but he was lazy and earned the income by literally falling into it! He didn't understand how to best utilize his talents. I invited him to work with me and gave him responsibility and an opportunity to develop his potential. He just couldn't do it. I noticed he'd sit at his desk, almost paralyzed. He didn't go after business, never looked for leads and never pursued listings. All his deals were actually the outcome from the referrals his mother passed along to him. Having an easy success lead him to believe he didn't have to do anything but strut around, boasting about the big bucks he earned. It was a "Hey, I make one hundred grand a year, I'm fabulous," small-picture mindset!

When placed in front of an opportunity that would require he use his own brainpower, he was scared and panicked. He just couldn't go out there and do it! After a while, I asked him to leave the company because he had an inflated ego.

Since everyone told him about his abundant potential, he was aware of his enormous capabilities. However, no one ever informed him that he was not using this potential until I confronted him. "You're not using your potential and if you're not going to, I don't need you here," I said. He was shocked and horrified to learn I was going to let him go and decided he would move on to another company.

Since I keep in touch with the other company, I often speak with him. Now he has admitted to me, "Tonja, you're right. I don't use my potential, but I can't figure out why!"

"That's easy," I responded.

"Well, tell me, why don't I use it?" he asked.

"It's easy for me to see, but you have to train your mind to help you figure it out," I replied.

"Tonja," he said, once again freezing his potential. "Aren't you going to give me the answer?"

"No," I said. "My answer is an opinion. Your answer is a conclusion based on exploration. You have to reach it on your own with your potential."

The lesson learned from this incident is that the mindset is the mechanism needed to master your own inner game of wealth. I like to consider wealth as a game of strategy, self-discovery, risk and focus. And if you focus your mind and center on affirmations, incantations and weeding out the thorns and thistles of barren people, you create your strategy to program your thoughts, setting yourself up to be successful at your game.

There is no doubt in my mind that multi-millionaires

differ from the rest of the people on the planet. They are positive, have "can do" attitudes and seem to really love what they do as well as do what they love. Their thinking is focused on solving problems and their actions are oriented towards achievement. Multi-millionaires shun neither accountability nor commitment. They take full responsibility for their lives.

Wealth-challenged individuals, on the other hand, always seem to have issues and problems cluttering their lives. They constantly focus on what they don't have, can't have or weren't given. Blame is the name of their game and they forever point a finger away from themselves, throwing guilt for their failings and poverty on other people or circumstances. They just refuse to take responsibility. Their glass is always half empty and they are locked into a language pattern of loss, lack and a "Woe is me, the eternal victim, unlucky and poor!" attitude.

Wealthy people have learned the formula for making money and have loaded it in their mindsets. It's not difficult to do. Decide right now that you want to be a positive, energetic, enthusiastic and successful person. Then look around and single out role models who exemplify what you want to become. If you don't see anyone in your circle of friends or sphere of influence, make it an obligation to get out and meet new friends to create a different sphere of influence. Associate with people who "speak multi-millionaire"! Learn and become fluent in their language. Always frequent self-confident, generous, humble, inspired and passionate "ladder climbers" who are actually going towards a destination. Tell yourself you can be one of them!

Surround yourself with examples of the wealth you desire. If you want a Ferrari Testarossa, go test drive one and hang a photo of the car above your desk to intensify your desire and motivate you. Once your Ferrari TR appetite is stimulated, your body and mind will help you strategize how to attain it.

Talk to yourself in positive affirmations daily—tell yourself you're a money magnet. Inform yourself that money flows into your life easily and effortlessly—design your own affirmations that will inspire, motivate and train your mindset to build the financial freedom and independence you want and deserve.

Always be mindful that you are what you think about and you become what you focus your energy on. Make the choice to channel your thoughts to where you *REALLY* want them to go.

Visualize your success; imagine you are watching the TV program *This is Your Life* in your mind's eye. See it as if it were already playing out. Envisioning yourself as if you're driving the Ferrari, having a multi-million dollar portfolio and enjoying the ideal relationship is a powerful mechanism. Accept that power, embrace it and believe it will give you all that you visualize. It can and it will, if it's what you truly want!

Start a crusade of self-discovery and learn about yourself—look at yourself in the mirror and get real. Find out what is holding you back. Eliminate the obstacles on your path. Ask yourself, "Who am I? What am I made of? Am I willing to do what it takes to become a casual millionaire? Now answer your questions! Attitude is 99 percent of success, so don't skimp here—train, discipline and motivate yourself. Just do it!

7

Linking With the Higher Power

It is my firm belief that nothing in life is possible without a spiritual connection, whether you choose to accept it or deny it! There are universal laws eternally in motion that design and govern how fate plays out. However, this does not imply that as human beings, we can kick off our shoes, rest on our laurels and wait for a Higher Power to drop from above all the fame and fortune we want. Sorry, but it just isn't going to happen—at least not that way!

Linking with the Higher Power is about letting the intentions you set to circulate in the universe. It's about having the certainty that the universe will never deny or refute what you want. If you truly desire a million dollars, the universe will not boycott your wish. Instead, it will allow you to continue "wanting" the big bucks *ad infinitum*!

Every structure and organism, human or otherwise, has a main bearing wall to maintain stability. In people, it's a spiritual foundation—the Higher Power. The universe is mastered by this Higher Power, who rules using spiritual energies. It is this Divine Force, interpreted as inspiration, which propels your consciousness towards a superior objective. As human beings, you were given the gift of free will at birth. Consequently, you are at liberty to set your intentions and pursue your objectives, using as nourishment the potent spiritual energies you share with the Higher Power! If properly utilized, these compelling forces can be of assistance to you during your journey towards acquiring all that you want.

When you make the decision to bond with the universe, you must be prepared to go beyond the familiar and take that all-important step into another dimension. Explore your new surroundings, discover what different path you can take to get you where you want to go, and make the decision to act on the choices you have set before you. In order to follow through on this plan, you have to learn how to unblock the barriers obstructing your existing thoughts and how to unlock the door, giving free passage to the positive things that surround you. First, you should recognize and accept their existence as affirming and inspiring elements, and second, you should be able to actually visualize them as they journey towards you. Open your mind and feel the effects of their entry in your body. Let them seep in, invade and energize you.

Set your intention to obtaining a better life, and believe beyond the slightest inkling of a doubt that you deserve to live the greatest life you can envision in your mind's eye. If you get in tune with your spiritual energy, and align yourself to the Divine Force in the universe, your life will take on a more evenhanded, harmonious and fulfilling nature. Take—or better still, *make* time to explore and become familiar with your spiritual resources. Look for and find your own unique connection with the Higher Power. Become acquainted with meditation and more importantly, learn how to "shut down" your systems in order to concentrate on your breathing. Get acquainted with your silence, become comfortable with your thoughts and enjoy the experience of a moment in your company.

As Mahatma Ghandi said, "In the attitude of silence the soul finds the path in clear light, and what is elusive and deceptive resolves itself into crystal clearness."

When discussing the Higher Power, I like to clarify that spirituality and religion are not necessarily identical. A person can be a spiritual being without attending structured religious service every week or quoting passages from the Sacred Books. Instead, as an alternative to ritualistic worship, spiritual people have their own personal connections to a Higher Consciousness. These individuals believe in a power that is greater than themselves, even though it operates through them. It's an omnipresent force that can be categorized as the existence of God, a Higher Power, a Higher Consciousness or a Divine Source, all of which can be interchanged as the core of spirituality.

When I speak about linking to the Higher Power, my thoughts focus on a truth, which implies that without this Divine Force, we are non-existent. Everything we do or accomplish here on earth, we do in agreement with the

Divine Plan. It is my belief that your plan and my plan were already formulated for us prior to our materializing in the physical plane. Although these plans were previously put together, it does not mean they are predestined. We always have the free will option, which gives us the power of choice and the authority to choose.

However, despite my confidence in the free will theory, I strongly believe there are certain contracts and agreements that our souls make before coming to earth. For instance, I engaged a marketing specialist for one of my companies and am certain that our souls met earlier, in a time in which it was decided we would come together in February of 2006 to collaborate on a project. This was to be my experience, and as a result of this occurrence, I am certain, a "contract" exists between me and my marketing specialist. In formulating this "agreement," we are now here, working together. Without the contract, we could not be involved in this professional relationship. Contracts differ in nature and time. Some are made to last a lifetime, some are drawn up to last ten minutes and others can be valid for years.

People sometimes ask me, "Tonja, how do you link the Higher Power and consciousness to the definition of what spirituality actually is?" In response, I tell them that I link it through personal growth and development. I think most individuals are accustomed to hearing about maturing and changing for the purpose of becoming the best people they can be. Often, I question why you would want to become that better individual. Do you simply do it because you heard about karma and are reluctant if not down right afraid you may be obliged to pay the karmic debt? Are you a good and virtuous person and therefore not subjected to the law of retribution? Why do you do it?

I think the answer lies in our souls' natural inclination and desire for growth—a change we hope will impede us from being obliged to experience the same lessons over and over. To demonstrate my point, I like to use relationships. When you're involved in a relationship and it has come to an end, you usually say, "I'm done with this person, period—I'm over it!" In reality, you're not done, because the next relationship you have may involve a different person but the same issue—plus, in a new relationship, you always pick up exactly where you left off!

This phenomenon occurs because you never really nursed back to health all the hurts that needed to be healed in order to be able to work through the issues that doomed the failed relationship in the first place. Therefore, whatever new relationship you jump into, the same problems will surface to interrupt it, unless there is complete healing. To heal, you must get in touch with your spiritual side.

I think creating a consciousness that says, "I'm really a small part of the world and the bigger part is my spiritual belief" is the connection I share with the greater planet and the immense good of everyone. As human beings, we are connected. Essentially, we are one entity; therefore, my actions have an effect on you and likewise your actions affect me. This is why it is important to observe the world in terms of interconnecting molecules of energy instead of focusing on the physicality of objects, which in reality are non-existent. For example, I sit in front of my desk. However, it has no life in the spiritual sphere, since it doesn't have an energy field. It is totally insignificant in the grand scheme of things. People unite, objects separate; people grow, objects remain static!

Two distinct components exist in all human beings: the ego self and the spiritual self. The former is linked to our wants and is not governed by the will of our consciousness or spiritual side. You can always distinguish between the *selves* because when you're in your spiritual element, you originate from a completely different place. You are usually in your spiritual self when you're presented with an issue or problematic circumstance to resolve and find yourself at peace with the decision you have made. On the other hand, if you're gnashing your teeth, struggling, anxious and in a situation of turmoil because you failed to satisfy the "I want my way" part of your being, you are typically in your ego self.

When the spirit and the ego try to enter into competition, there is no fair contest, because the spirit will forever triumph. The Higher Power always consents to choice, allowing you the decision to have what you want and be who you want to be. You may have to repeat the lesson over again before it feels right, but that's your choice.

I believe that when you're on a path to increasing prosperity, you have to understand that the wealth you are generating is being created for the greater good of the planet, and is not your exclusive property. In fact, you accumulate wealth primarily as a means of accomplishing great things for the collective good. In order to create enormous wealth, your mind has to be ready to expand into the realm of consciousness that says, "I know I am more than my ego. I know I have a greater purpose while I'm here on this planet and I know my consciousness has to support all that the greater purpose is. This means I might have to grow and develop my consciousness, and be able to assume more responsibility for the life I have and for the experiences dominating my mind. The point is, if you never change your consciousness, you will never modify any of your experiences. That is stagnation.

As children, most of us were taught there is a God. His place of location is set in the sky, and everyone looked up, believing a Divine Source was gazing down to control us and to punish those who misbehaved! God was given a male gender and was "designed" as an elderly gentleman with a lush, white beard!

Today, I don't believe God has a gender and resides up in the sky, beyond the sun, moon and stars. Instead, it is my firm conviction that God, an Omnipresent Force, is everywhere. And the presence of God intensifies as I open myself to the flow of this Omnipresence in my life. Often, we lose ourselves in trying to analyze God, missing the point. Instead, we should be spending our time identifying with the spirit and learning who we are in relationship to the universe.

I remember gazing up at the sky, saying, "God is there! That's God. Okay! So, what exactly does that all mean? I guess it means I'm supposed to be good!" Now, I realize it doesn't center on my being good. Actually, the focus is elsewhere. If I want to be everything I came to this world to become, then I have to make a conscious effort to learn how to accomplish my purpose. We all have a singular role to play and a unique script to recite. It is designed to complement our higher purpose and lead us to the giving we are here to do. Your reason to be equates with developing yourself and being of service to others. It's about contribution. This charitable virtue puts you in coalition with the Divine Force and consequently balances the power between your will and your higher being. If you truly have not experienced the immense power of giving, you are not yet connected to your spiritual persona.

As Buddha said, "If you knew what I know about the power of giving, you would not let a single meal pass without sharing it in some way." He uses the metaphor of meal sharing, Christians practice the *tithing* and Jews have the tradition of the *tzedakah*. It is one and the same, regardless of the rhetoric. It's about moral accountability—offering to others, both before and after you have received.

When you connect to a spiritual force and believe in a Higher Being, you make yourself available to receive more opportunities and varied experiences. You unbolt the doors and open yourself up to a whole different way of thinking and feeling. This results in the birth of new experiences. And in creating these new experiences, you gain a deeper understanding of spirituality.

In the previous chapter, I spoke about affirmations and the positive effect they have on reaching objectives. I define affirmations as affirmative prayer, because basically, they are a way of bringing your prayer into consciousness and acting as if it is already known. Mahatma Ghandi said it best when he noted, "Prayer is not an old woman's idle amusement. Properly understood and applied, it is the most potent instrument of action." Prayer is communication. It is a dialogue between our selves and the Divine Power.

I am a believer in Religious Science, which is a faith based on philosophy and science that employs tangible theories, easily demonstrated and applicable for the strengthening of man's relationship to the universe and the general betterment of life. It is intended to enlarge consciousness by emphasizing a spiritual link.

Religious Science also provides a scientific method for making choices that lead you towards what you want and away from what you don't want. When you have established a spiritual connection you truly believe in, you will open up and set yourself up for success. Which spiritual belief you choose—Christianity, Judaism, Islam, Buddhism, all of them, two of them or something else—is insignificant in the big picture. What is important is your believe in a Superior Power and not necessarily a god-person.

As the Dalai Lama said, "This is my simple religion—there is no need for temples; no need for complicated philosophy. Our own brain, our own heart is our temple; the philosophy is kindness." He made it relatively simple to grasp. Personally, I always have a total awareness of the presence of God. I know the energy that encourages me to grow and change is actually the Divine Omnipresence. This process of personal evolution aligns me with the Divine Force, enabling me to achieve my objectives with less effort. I keep moving in a higher realm and do what I like doing. And as I strive to do what I truly enjoy doing, I notice my prosperity increases.

Every outcome depends on your thought process. Once again, I'll use one of my favorite concepts, "What you think about, you bring about," to illustrate my point. I have heard people deny the existence of God because as they say, "God has never done anything for me." I remember a conversation I had with someone on this topic and I can still hear the litany of laments. "Look at my life. I'm surrounded by death and bad circumstances. It's one thing after another. Before I have time to recover, something bad happens again. Therefore, how can you tell me there is a God and expect me to believe in a Divine Plan when my life is so horrible? How can any universal force permit pain and suffering on this planet and not do anything to alleviate it?"

This is a difficult question to answer, just like the pointless tragedy of 9/11. When the terrorists killed and destroyed, many people said, "If there is truly a Superior Universal Power, how can this slaughter of innocent victims have occurred without being stopped?" I think many individuals have a mistaken concept of the identity of the Divine Power. They cannot put a finger on whom and what this Higher Force is all about. And what they fail to recognize is the existence of free will and choice. God did not create terrorism, man did. God did not force anyone to pilot an airplane into the World Trade Center—man drove it, in accordance with his own will. Therefore, to place blame on the Higher Power or to refute the existence of God is not an answer to the forever debated "If there is a God, why wasn't this catastrophe prohibited from happening?" question.

What many doubters and cynics fail to realize is that even disbelieving is a belief. When people say, "I don't believe in God or in a Higher Power," in essence, they are connecting with something that still activates their spiritual side. To reason is to believe and even die-hard atheists have a belief in a refusal to believe. That in itself is a belief.

People in general need to believe in a "special presence," something or someone superior to us who is accountable for the planet. We search for answers, often groping in the darkness because we want to know who created us and who was responsible for the Universal Master Plan. It's too big and too complicated for a simple answer. Were Adam and Eve the original parents of humanity? If not, who was responsible for creation? Who actually put together the design of the world as we know it?

We realize from early on, as children, that there is a Superior Force, but as we mature, we question not only how it all came to be but also how it continues. The striving is toward acquiring information and gaining awareness of our parts in all this immensity.

Linking with the Spiritual Intelligence is a way of setting in motion your thought process, to allow you to arrive at the conclusion that the universal creation is part of the big picture. It has a deeper meaning and an understanding that is hard to articulate because it is so very personal and subjective. You can struggle with it for years or you can get it instantly. Try this experiment. When you wake up in the morning, look into a mirror, make direct eye contact and connect to your inner spirit. Concentrate, focus and center your gaze. You will notice that beyond your eyes, there is much more than your eyes. Now, take it a step further. The next time you're standing in line, waiting to order a latte, take a moment to gaze into the eyes of the barista. Perhaps at a first glance, you'll murmur to yourself, "I really don't care for that person. I don't like the way he or she looks." Well, take a real look. Go beyond the surface. Fix and hold your gaze on the eyes for thirty seconds. Go beyond the color or shape. You will be amazed to discover that a connection is inevitable and unavoidable. And you will come away with a totally different feeling about that individual.

I believe this connection happens because the God inside of us recognizes the God inside of them. "God created man in His image. In the image of God he created him"—that's how it's explained in Genesis 1:27.

Once you become familiar with the non-judgmental nature of spirituality and realize that it's not about criticizing or evaluating another, you'll hear yourself saying, "I accept you for who you are. I accept you in all things because my purpose here in the universe is not to judge you. I may choose not to be in your presence as a result of a particular behavior or circumstance, but I don't pass judgment on that matter or condition, because if I sit as judge, I render judgment on myself and I am neither here in the role of judge nor do I care to be judged."

This introspection gives us an opportunity to decide who we want to become in the bigger picture, how we want to live our lives and what role we envision for spirituality as it relates to us on a personal level. It also leads us to visualize how we want spirituality to manifest itself in our lives.

Some people can witness the birth of spirituality while eating a cheeseburger. They could bite down and feel a bolting, life-altering awakening that makes them exclaim, "Oh, my God! I just realized I'm a spiritual being enjoying a human experience." Others may arrive through a deeper process. They may have vocational callings to religious life, as either priests, nuns, deacons, rabbis or ministers. Still others, like Deepak Chopra, sponsor meditation groups and run centers for holistic body, mind and spirit well-being. This bears evidence that spirituality manifests itself in diverse ways in different people. However, there is one common factor—they all have well-delineated spiritual connections. There is no separation among mankind—no you and me, but we. Everyone is one with the Divine Power. If there is no division, whatever you choose to do affects me and conversely, whatever I decide to do affects you. Therefore, on some level, conscious or otherwise, the actions of a few greatly influence the universe.

The 9/11 World Trade Center massacre was a powerful burden of proof, because it demonstrated without a shadow of doubt how the choices of a handful of humanity devastated and changed an entire planet forever. The families involved and their families and friends and every human being around them were drastically affected, making the catastrophic episode a global disaster. President Bush, Pope John Paul II, Maryanne Williamson, Deepak Chopra, the Dalai Lama and spiritual leaders around the world united in prayer.

In recognizing how the actions of a few can affect the entire human population, it is difficult to grasp why some individuals are called upon to experience so much pain whereas others sail though life almost untouched. What fails to sink in sometimes is not why we suffer, but what lesson we learned or what message we received from the sad event. How did it make us a better person for having endured and overcome?

People ask me all the time, "Tonja, how on earth did you get to become a multi-millionaire when you have such a background of adverse circumstances?" It's an interesting observation. Actually, an aura of loss has clouded my life from early on. I was born surrounded by the experiences of death. My mother passed away when I was two months old and I was raised by my grandmother, whom I always called Mom. When I was still a teenager, my best friend committed suicide. Shortly thereafter, I buried my grandmother, then my father, and finally my grandfather, and I remained alone.

When I look back, I realize that since I first saw the light of day, the circumstances of my life revolve around and fit into a clearly delineated pattern of loss. However, I interpret it as a pattern of growth. I feel these were occurrences my soul had to experience, live through, understand and survive. It was part of my journey. I also believe we experience many lifetimes and I'm certain that in my former lives, I resolved issues and am here now to continue the healing process with other concerns. Loss was always a major player in my life. I didn't seek it out—it found me. However, despite the darkness, I never lost my way. Instead, I turned into the light and discovered the truth.

To get where I am today, I listened to my consciousness whispering to reassure me, "There is no loss." I learned acceptance. Anything that happens is okay because it was meant to be, for a better good, whether or not we are able to see it in any given moment.

I remember the day my mom passed away. Everyone was so despondent and in tears. I was saddened also, but I conquered my pain by focusing on where her new destination had taken her. I was convinced she was in a better place and felt elated for her, knowing she was at peace and that her agony had been silenced. Looking from a different perspective,

I knew it was all part of the Master Plan. It was because it was supposed to be. Death is not necessarily synonymous with the end; it can lead to surprising alternatives. Yes, we miss our loved ones, but holding on is forfeiting the possibilities of life.

I had two dogs, one for 18 years and the other for 16. When they passed on a couple of years ago, the loss was so draining; I thought I would never recover from the pain. Then, all of a sudden, while I was taking a walk, on my path was placed the cutest looking, gray-colored Italian greyhound. She was adorable. I looked into her eyes and it was love at first sight. Today, I have three beautiful dogs. And though I thought I would never recover from my loss, I did. I went forward to love and raise three new beautiful creatures who found the TLC they needed in that moment.

The old saying that "time heals all wounds" actually has a thread of truth. It is not time in the physical sense, but I believe it's time in understanding, time in growth and time in consciousness. When you're prepared to pass through it and ready to get over it, you will. Just like that. It can and sometimes does happen in a split second. There I was and there stood the little greyhound. What a connection!

I also believe you are never given a burden without the strength to endure and survive. Think about it. It's part of the package. Lessons are taught when we are available and willing to learn. We all have the ability to absorb what we are given, though we don't always make the choice to do so. It's unfortunate, because we pass up an opportunity to become a better person.

This is carried over also in business. The same connection

exists. Everyone has the potential to earn money and to be happy. The question is, will you choose to?

As a human being, you have two components: a spiritual self and an ego self. The spiritual connection keeps you on track. Many times, the ego mind takes over and floods the consciousness with chaotic thoughts, feelings and beliefs. When you're capable of directing the ego mind to stop blocking traffic and move out of the way, and when you're able to center yourself either in quiet meditation, prayer or walking reflection, you will be able to unite with the consciousness of your Higher Power. In addition, you will settle in and relax in the certainty of knowing what you really feel about something, someone or a decision taken. At this point, you can establish a connection with your own source and spirit, a bond that can assist you in finding the answers to many of your questions. In turn, these answers will guide you through your journey. This guidance is more concrete, unyielding and sound than the advice and opinions of those who surround you. If you pause a moment to listen you will be amazed at the power you hold within your mind.

If you pay attention, you will be able to distinguish between the voice of your Higher Power and that of your ego mind. The sounds and feelings are very distinct. I know exactly when I'm in my ego because it's extremely flippant, and when I'm absorbed in my own spiritual connection, there's a spreading aura of peace, a total calming, an awareness that tells me, "This is it!"

With the ego, there's a push and pull, besides a justification. And there's all the mind chatter, repeating and echoing what the ego wants and needs to hear. The ego craves the "snap of a finger" pleasure—the "I want it now" instant gratification. Without accountability or reference to consequence, it shouts, "Yes! Yes! Yes! Buy that new car even though you can't afford to pay for it right now. Why not? You deserve it!"

The spiritual consciousness comes back with, "Do you really need this car? Isn't there a more opportune time to buy a new car? Think about it!"

The ego snaps in defense: "Ah, don't think about that! Forget it. Just go ahead and get it. You know you want it. You'll really look cool driving around in it! Just think how good you're going to feel! Why wait?"

Stop the ego-spiritual, verbal mental battle. Take a few deep breaths and make a decision to drop the rash, instant gratification choice pushing you to "Go, ego, get it and drive away!" Listening to the ego will not allow you to hear the truth. You'll just sign on the dotted line, drive off and get a momentary spurt of exhilaration soon to subside when the consequence of your decision kicks in.

This verbal mental battle is a scuffle, a tug-of-war between the ego and the spirit. The ego pushes to win, playing underhandedly, forcing you to see the pleasure-receiving side only, because the last thing it wants is to be set in second place or ignored. If the ego is disregarded or put on hold, it loses its job and has nothing to do. Therefore, the ego tries its best to entice you into saying, "Yeah, let's go for it. I want instant gratification! I want it and I want it now!"

This is what occurs much too frequently in people's professional affairs, causing disastrous financial situations. They get on track and decide it's time to make a difference. In good faith, they make a commitment and suddenly they switch into reverse and slip twenty steps backward because they are not able to resist the temptation for on-the-spot indulgence. They want what they want when they want it—once again siding with the smooth talking, pleasure promising ego. Aware that they are choosing unwisely, they go for it anyway. The common sense, "I shouldn't buy that now because if I hold out for two more months, conditions would differ and I'd be in a better position to do it" alternative is totally overlooked. As a result of their faulty decision, they're set back five or ten years and forced to deal with avoidable consequences for their reckless actions.

In denial, they justify their foolishness, saying, "Oh, you know, even though this happened, I don't regret it. I got what I wanted. I felt great and anyway, it'll be okay! So what's the big deal? I'm driving my dream car and having a good time!"

Leave the ego alone. You will feel a rush of power when you step into your own personal power, which springs forth the moment you connect with the Higher Source. Establish a routine that outlines how you nurture yourself spiritually— ask yourself, "What can I do to grow, deepen and expand my spiritual consciousness and be aligned more intensely with the Higher Power? Don't yank out your hair searching for the right answer. There are no correct answers and no textbook guidelines except what works for you. The task involves discovering what exactly that is.

I'll share a routine that benefits me. Every morning, I meditate. I spend 45 minutes clearing my mind and preparing myself for the day's activities ahead of me. Usually, I read passages that focus on spiritual growth and development, which help me examine myself and determine what path my journey is taking. I select writings that stimulate my thinking to pursue new possibilities and reflect on different options I never considered previously. Perhaps there is another idea, a better theory or a more productive way to do something that I have not yet explored. And as I read and meditate, my mind expands, encouraging me to question how if there is another concept aside from the universal picture, how do I give importance to that big picture in my little world? The answer involves stepping out of my little world and joining the big world!

An example of "big world participation" is contribution. People say, "I'll give! I'll give! I'll give—when I start making money!" Instead, the giving should occur before the earning. If you need a mantra for meditation, make the words of St. Francis of Assisi yours: "For it is in giving that we receive"— and not in receiving that we give!

Contribution does not always equate with a monetary figure. Giving involves consideration for and sharing with others. Just a simple act of thoughtfulness, like shutting the faucet while brushing your teeth to conserve water, is an act of kindness towards the people we share the planet with. Take the time to turn the lights off and to recycle—this signifies being a part of the big picture and stepping into the big world. The planet is not here to accommodate one or two generations, it's here until the Divine Power decides otherwise.

How do we participate in the big picture? How do we look after each other? We nurture by setting up a discipline that keeps us connected and by surrounding ourselves with people who are of like mind. It's difficult to be on a path toward spiritual and financial development when those around you are not moving in the same direction.

If your spiritual belief is Judaism, immerse yourself in the Jewish culture. Read the *Torah* or the *Kabala*. If it's Christianity, pick up the *Holy Bible*. If it's Islam, take in hand the *Qur'an*. If Buddhism is your conviction, read the Dalai Lama's thoughts. If your belief is not as formal, fine, read some of the modern day thinkers or the books by Deepak Chopra and Wayne Dyer—or write your own meditation. Likewise, surround yourself with individuals who share your belief system. This spiritual bonding will solidify your faith and allow you to integrate it into your consciousness. Whatever identity your belief has, if it is going to contribute to your spiritual expansion, it has to be developed, cultivated and nourished.

Ever since I was a child, I always had a strong spiritual connection, which was often evidenced in the poetry I wrote. However, I never fully understood the power and intensity of that relationship until later on. One of my training companies was showing remarkable profits until the 9/11 act of terrorism. Following the attack on the World Trade Center, every company I had a contract with for corporate and sales training either pulled out or put their business projects on hold, uncertain of the outcome on the global economy. All budgets were frozen and I was unable to sell my training to anyone.

I was already in an office lease with an option to purchase. In addition, there was a provision that gave me the opportunity to sublet the property. I exercised my option and sublet it. However, the landlord still sued me for the entire amount of the lease—a sum which amounted to $400,000.

I dissolved the company. It was a painful ego event and extremely difficult to do. I saw it coming. My intuition alerted me and although I had an opportunity to get out of it earlier, before it went totally down, my ego just wouldn't let me. And amazingly, I did not like the business. I was not passionate about what I was doing! However, I did it solely because I thought it was the thing to do and once I had committed to it, I refused to quit! My ego was guiding my life.

People around me saw the signs and kept saying, "Tonja, why are you doing that? Why don't you let it go?" Best of all, I had an inkling that I totally ignored. At the time, I was selling real estate and was involved in my own transactions to fund my corporate sales training company. I was doing something I loved on the side to subsidize the company and employees I was caught up in full time and didn't like! The message was loud and clear, but I couldn't hear it because the voice of my burly ego was too overpowering. I felt I started the company and I had to stay and make it work. My ego boss was at the helm.

A friend called me and said, "Tonja, you're so good in real estate. Look at the great investments you have. It's apparent this is your world—so why are you persisting in a business you dislike?" When I told her, "I'm doing it because I said I was going to do it," she replied, "Tonja, that's the stupidest thing I've ever heard! Where have you been? Haven't you heard about choice? Just because you liked something in one moment doesn't mean you have to like it and keep doing it in another moment. That's what life is all about. You get to consider options; you get to seize new opportunities. You have the possibility to continually redesign your life and you stay in the outdated environment. Tonja, success depends on your openness to change."

Obviously, at this point in time, I was not aligned with change. My ego had me barricaded and following a flippant and narrow path. As a result, I continued to struggle over my debt with the landlord, who pursued the $400,000. He went full speed ahead and opted to sue me. I phoned him and said, "Listen, Dan, can we negotiate a settlement? You have not lost any funds. I sublet the property. Money is coming in! How about if I pay you $50,000 over a period of time? If you don't accept this deal, I'll have no choice but to file for bankruptcy."

"No, Tonja," he responded, "I don't think you'll ever file a bankruptcy. You just don't have that type of personality!"

"Dan," I said, "you're really not leaving me any alternatives. I'm being up-front with you. This is the situation."

"Tonja," he replied, "I find it hard to believe you! I think you have more money and can bail yourself out of this one! You should just pay me!"

"Dan," I said, "I'm telling you the truth. I don't have the money!"

Dan just refused to believe that I couldn't handle my financial responsibility. Consequently, he left me no choice but to file for bankruptcy. Going down to the bankruptcy court and filing was the most humbling experience of my life. My ego was stomped on and discarded.

I remember sitting in court with people who were discharging $5,000 worth of debt. And here I was, with perfect credit, no credit card debt—but a $400,000 office lease to discharge! I thought to myself, "I've always been a successful negotiator. I don't want to file this bankruptcy." I knew Dan did not lose any money and I questioned, "What is the message here? What is the meaning behind this experience? Why is this happening to me, and how am I supposed to profit from this?"

There was no doubt in my mind—my bankruptcy demonstrated the existence of a bigger picture. It was not just about dollars and cents. Instead, there was a lot more to it. Before this experience, my life was focused on making money—and I did. Then, some obstacle would materialize to interrupt the flow. I noticed that although I made money, I never made a difference! And what I really wanted, what circled in my mind, what was at the core of my being, was my passionate intention to make "the difference."

I realized this was not about money. This was about being taught a lesson—but more importantly, it was about stumbling into a valuable learning experience that confirmed I should do what I love doing and stop getting caught up in the opinions of others regarding how I should live my life! This was the beginning of a life-altering turning point.

When I faced the lease issue with Dan, people said to me, "Tonja, reimburse him the full payment for his lease. Do whatever it takes to settle this matter. Make an arrangement to shell out the $400,000 in one way or another and save your credit."

Instead of taking the seemingly good advice, I chose to handle it in the way I thought was best. For the first time, I did what I wanted to do. I based my decision on what I personally felt was the right path for me to follow. I knew I had offered Dan a fair agreement and I was prepared to go beyond my comfort zone. When my plan was met with little success, I thought, "Okay. This is what I said I was going to do and after wasting time and energy, struggling with it for over a year, it feels right to me. I'll just take that path."

I did, and filed the bankruptcy, fully aware I could never renege on it. Four months later, my bankruptcy was discharged. The following day, I made a million dollars. Within six months, my net worth amounted to over $36,000,000! There I was, just six months after I filed for bankruptcy, with a large fortune!

Thinking about it, I said to myself, "How ironic. I struggled for such a long time to keep something together financially, yet the second I made the choice to let it go and do what I really wanted to do, which was real estate, everything fell into place."

In a certain sense, we are the master designers of our own destinies, in accordance with the Higher Power. "God does not change the condition of any people unless they themselves make the decision to change," as it says in *Qur'an Sura 13; Thunder.*

I understood that my spiritual connection lead me to listen, to be observant, to be aware and to interpret all the signs that revealed what my soul-print was all about. They were clearly evident and told me I was not intentioned to run a training company. Once I began to read my spiritual floor plan, I moved ahead and formed over ten companies, all related to real estate and real estate-related activities. I realized that my power and strength were reinforced in the ability to "know when to hold 'em and when to fold 'em," as Kenny Rogers sang.

Although I deliberated, my spiritual connection with the Divine Will made me aware that I really did not have another option. That was the way it had to be—and that was the way it was. In life, there are doors that open easily to allow a smooth walk through and there are doors that are resistant and prohibit an effortless passage. However, if you have to force a door open to continue your journey, you're proceeding in the wrong direction. The ego will not comply with that concept, because it neither refuses a challenge even if it's counterproductive nor turns away from an obstacle, being far too proud and self-centered to admit making a less–than-perfect choice. Consequently, many times you fail.

I have learned from my own spiritual journey to walk through a door that opens easily and effortlessly and explore the vast world that lies beyond. And if I am obliged to push and shove, I'll just postpone my walk through until I can swing it open with ease.

However, prior to my spiritual connection with the Higher Power, I would struggle and force the door, believing with every thrust that negotiating was really about figuring out who would get the ego thrilling "Yes" first. Then, I realized it was about helping others get what they want. It had nothing to do with what I could get and all to do with what I could give.

This change represented the most essential growing experience in my life. It showed me the importance of listening to my inner voice. The longer you fight it, the more miserable and un-gratifying your life will become and the longer it will take to turn it around. If you continually repress your interior energy and stubbornly contradict your inner inclination, you are fighting the spiritual guidance that is coming to you. Stop resisting and get in the flow. Flip the script—whatever you are thinking or doing, steer it back on course. Focus on what you want, on what you know is right for you in any given moment. Just don't live to avoid what you don't want. Center your intention and focus on your spiritual connection because this link with the Higher Power is the energy that will fuel your intentions and lead you on a journey to personal and financial prosperity.

According to Oprah Winfrey, "It isn't until you come to a spiritual understanding of who you are—not necessarily a religious feeling, but a deep down, the spirit within—that you begin take control!"

8

Taking Action: Getting Down to Business

According to one of the most pre-eminent multi-millionaires, Walt Disney, "If you can dream it, you can do it." I agree and believe that if your intention for success involves making serious positive changes, you must capitalize on your potential and commitment in order to attain a positive outcome. Get down to business. Assess the changes you want to implement. Always be aware that a major contributing factor to success is time management. However, despite the words "time management," we are incapable of actually managing the hours in our day. Time passes at a steady pace, neither taking into account nor honoring the wishes of those who are subject to its rapid course. If you stop to think about it, you will realize that our moments in time are truly unmanageable and irrepressible because time is a tool of the Higher Power. It takes orders from the Divine Will, its sole manager.

Often, when I speak about time management in my seminars, people approach me afterwards and ask, "Tonja, if we cannot manage time, what's the point of believing that success in business is dependent on time management?"

It's a good observation. "Well," I say, "By time management, I mean managing your thoughts and activities so that your day is planned without wasting time. Basically, the idea is to make good use of the time you have."

I think Leonardo DaVinci summed it up in an interesting way: "One can have no smaller or greater mastery than mastery of oneself."

Most people will say, "But, Tonja, I never have enough time to get everything I set out to accomplish! How can I make changes to improve? And how can I make more time in my day?"

Unfortunately, much as we would all love the luxury of a 30-hour day, we cannot increase the minutes in an hour or the hours in a day. However, it is possible to create the illusion of more time by increasing your productivity level and designing your day to get more done in the time you do have. If you observe successful people, you will notice that they handle more than most individuals and achieve a higher percentage of their objectives, yet they live in the same 24-hour day as you do.

In reality, time management is self-governance. Corporations, be they Fortune 500 companies or small firms, have skillfully trained management teams to oversee staff and make certain procedures and policies are efficiently implemented for employee retention and profit gain. Well, the same talent and proficiency required to manage others can be utilized to manage ourselves.

I have found in my personal experiences that the key to productive self-management is to learn how to plan, organize, assign responsibilities, be in command and be able to identify the time wasting trends that leave us depleted of energy and our daily tasks uncompleted.

Another major factor in self-management is being able to take action on your intention. This requires replenishing your energy resources by getting and staying physically fit. If you're not at your physical best, your mental state will pay the penalty—your attention span will waver and your concentration quotient will take a dive. This is a recipe for failure! There is, however, a flip slide formula that will take you on a successful path. I have a daily routine I'm committed to that recharges my physical and mental batteries and gets me moving.

After my meditation, I like to incorporate some form of aerobic exercise into my day. Usually, I walk. I find the rhythmic movement powers my body, stimulating my creative juices, which in turn empower my mind. It sharpens my thinking and sets my general pace at a higher speed, allowing me to accomplish more in less time. While my body is being revitalized with each step I take, my mind is diligently at work, grabbing the ideas generated by my spiritual connection and spinning them into a plan I will put in action that very day.

In order to fine tune myself to keep pace with my plan, I review in my mind the most important things I need to consider if I want to use my time wisely and productively. As previously mentioned, my connection to the Higher Power is my primary energy source. It motivates, inspires, nourishes and thrusts me forward to meet the day's challenges head on, convinced I'll accomplish my objectives.

Once the spirit and mind are nurtured, it's important to take care of the body. Study your dietary habits and eliminate the sugary foods and caffeine-loaded beverages that drain your energy and give you a momentary false high, rendering you a major obstacle to your own productivity.

In one of my training seminars, I conducted a little experiment. I asked people to stop drinking caffeine and to quit smoking. "Do it right now," I said. "Make it a split-second decision and take immediate action! Then, monitor your energy for ninety days and observe how you feel during the course of each day."

I have discovered that most individuals fail to achieve their objectives because they continue to feed their systems with toxic substances that produce false energy, with little resistance and a short life span. The tobacco and caffeine overload creates a bogus spurt of energy that is gone in the blink of an eye, leaving you sapped, exhausted and useless.

This self-improvement plan is an essential part of the time management deal. It encourages you step on it and take action to change a situation or condition that is holding you back. Dr. Phil is right on target when he says to his audience, "If you want more, you have to require more from yourself."

If you want to gain optimum benefits from your potential, you need to be in the best condition possible. Making the decision and choosing to move forward, although rather difficult actions, add to your life in a significant way, helping you to expand time. The larger your source of healthy energy, the longer you can keep going. Your day will start earlier and end later, because energized from your fitness routine and dietary changes, your resources power you longer.

Often I see some of the twenty-somethings in my office totally wiped out by midday. Amazed, I think to myself, "I can run circles around these young and potentially vital kids without even getting winded!" Unfortunately, they are handicapped by their own faulty choices.

My day starts at 4:15 a.m. After I get my blood flowing through my body and mind by running through my mental, physical and spiritual exercises, I'm fueled for my intention-productive day.

I think it is very important to consider the foundational component when building your plan for success. You would never put up a house without first laying a solid foundation. Therefore, to construct your action plan for success, you really need to have a firm support structure, which starts with spirituality. Then, you must move on to fostering the physical component. It's about commitment, it's about self-obligation and it's about discipline!

Once you've assumed the responsibility for personal betterment, I recommend you expand time by setting your alarm an hour earlier, even if you're greeted by a tired feeling when your eyes finally open to full capacity. And tired you will be, because most people will feel exhausted. Don't focus on the tiredness. Instead, swing your legs off the bed, set your feet on the floor, take a deep breath and stand up. Resist the temptation to jump back between the sheets for that famous extra five minutes that mysteriously spreads into an hour. Go to your treadmill or cycle, go to the health club or fitness center or go outside for a walk. Get some fresh air into your lungs. Get empowered and get your body and mind moving.

If you really can't get your motor running, go to Starbucks, order a small latte or preferably a large glass of orange juice and grab a personal and professional self-help book to learn what you can do to improve your quality of life and your business, whether it's real estate, IT, marketing, legal or medical. If you're not exercising or meditating, spend the extra hour reading something that influences you positively and motivates you to take a new path on your professional journey.

If you are willing to give yourself a more results-oriented start off early in the day, it will enhance motivation, create incentive and build the solid foundation which is the core of any successful endeavor.

Another important element is the wise usage of allotted time. Usually I look at salespeople, as they seem to be a great segment of the working world. And I find that most individuals are reactive. Everything is based on an instinctive, knee-jerk plan of action or strategy. However, most events need to be scheduled. You have to stabilize a timetable for making calls and another for receiving them.

People tend to give precedence to the things they like to do as opposed to what they need to do. To overcome this roadblock, I advise people to write an agenda and organize it into a schedule. To facilitate scheduling, prioritize. Make a list of the most important matters and urgent matters that need your immediate attention. Learn to distinguish between what's urgent and important, what's urgent and unimportant, what's important and urgent, and what's neither important nor urgent—and take action accordingly.

This line of attack will provide you with valuable input regarding what you actually need to address. Obviously, you don't waste time on things that either can wait or are so low on your priority list that they can easily be postponed, if not overlooked for more pressing matters.

I tell my staff to create a time log to monitor their activities. This provides assurance they're not only utilizing their hours wisely, but they're not wasting time. Not long ago, I conducted one of my experiments. I had all the people in my office chart their activities for five consecutive business days. They were told to write down every single thing they did and the time in which it occurred. Everything was to be recorded, including rest room trips, lunch breaks and midmorning pauses. At the end of the week, they had an eye-opening experience when they saw in black and white how much of their day was actually wasted.

One of my salesmen told me, "Tonja, I'm so enormously and incredibly busy. I can't handle anything else!"

I thought to myself, "You can't handle what you have, yet I see you goofing off all the time."

At the end of the week, he was shocked by the entries on his time log. "My God, Tonja," he said, "I can't believe what I see here! When I filled it in honestly, I was in for an enlightening experience. I spent most of my time chatting—talking about the past weekend or my evening or even my life experiences. And I discovered that I spent more time talking to people in the office than to clients on the phone. I had absolutely no idea I was wasting so much time."

"Well, shocking to me," I responded.

When you conscientiously do a time log, it's a very useful tool in time management. It is also amusing to track the "cheating factor"! Many people either go into convenient denial or just fudge on it. They'll erase and scribble over the timeline. Although it sometimes gets a chuckle out of me, I often think that if you undertake an exercise to improve the quality of your life and your finances, don't camouflage the results by cheating. It's just another way to waste more time.

Take a real good look at yourself as a person and make the decision to be open to seeing what you see and accepting what you see. Like in a 12-step program, acceptance is your first step. If you can't or won't accept the existence of a failing, you will never be able to manage and overcome it. However, if you're serious about improving, you have to define what you're dealing with, acknowledge it and put a plan of action in place that will allow you to create the necessary steps to become more prosperous.

Once again, the most important factors are self-management and time management, because if you cannot manage your time, other people will do it. And obviously, they will do it in a way that benefits them, not you! One of things I do personally and strongly encourage is to use driving time for phone meetings. I have a hands-free headset for my cell phone, and when I'm in the car during rush hour traffic or traveling long distances, I turn the time productive by answering questions, doing consulting, getting briefed from my office and doing whatever I can to move my day forward.

I even schedule my social calls during "freeway experiences." In fact, all my friends know my car schedules and ring me accordingly when they want to link up for a chat. Otherwise, they don't phone because they know I'm not available. The interesting point here is that most of my friends are the same way. They are busy professionals who value their time as much as I do. So, telephone socializing is a freeway commuting happy hour.

My first suggestion for renovating your time management plan is to identify where, how and why you are wasting time. Then, repair the defects. Find out what you can eliminate or change to gain more time. I compare it to a leaky faucet. If your water bill is increasing every month but your consumption of water remains the same, something is wrong. What do you do? You certainly don't throw up your arms in surrender and increase the amount on your check every month. Instead, you face the issue, locate the leaky faucet responsible for the waste and repair it.

Now, apply the same principle to your costly "time leak." Examine your day, find where and why your time is seeping out on you and fix it to give yourself more time. In addition, challenge yourself to be as productive as possible from sunrise to sunset. And if you find yourself at a loss for what to do, don't panic.

Productivity is not always one and the same with a high busy quotient. For some individuals, productivity is taking time to think, investigate, explore and discover what exactly their next move is. They spend time observing their business, surveying their career path, perhaps from a different perspective and just sitting down to think about new strategies to implement for profit growth.

I had a gentleman working for me not long ago who was from St. Petersburg, Florida. He was the office snail. Everyone would beat him to their cars at lunchtime by ten minutes. Taking into consideration that there are usually four trips to the parking area per day, at the end of the week, he was in the red 40 minutes a day. At the end of the workweek, he had wasted 3.33 hours of quality time.

Once you locate the source of your waste, challenge yourself to do something about it by motivating yourself to be more productive. Accelerate the speed of your productivity. Don't move through the day fueled by a "Florida stroll" mentality that leaves you still in the parking lot when everyone else is diligently at work in the office! Quicken your pace; walk, don't meander through the day. If you're slow, you'll get less done. Treat your life like a record played at a faster speed. Speed generates energy and energy generates movement. The more you set your body in motion, the more momentum you gain, because the emotion of movement creates the momentum. In turn, movement creates more movement.

Speed up. Walk faster and step forward with purpose. People laugh when I tell them to do this. "My God, Tonja," I hear over and over again, "you walk so fast. Whenever we go out to an airport to preview properties, we can hardly keep pace without getting winded!"

"Well," I respond, "I've got a time schedule. I'm flying in. I'm looking at properties for an hour and a half with a Realtor and then I've got to get back and catch a flight out."

All of this means I don't have time to waste, waltzing through my day like I'm promenading on a fashion runway. I need to rent a car, hit the road and jump from one property to another—I need to hurry up! Breathlessly, my colleagues tell me, "Tonja, we feel like we have to run to keep up with you!"

"The only reason you feel you have to run to keep up is because you haven't conditioned yourself to operate at a faster speed," I respond.

When you condition yourself to operate at maximum speed to accomplish things, your energy pushes you forward, making it difficult for most people to keep your pace. You will hear them say, "God, I wish I could do that!"

Stop right there! Don't just wish it—live it. Make it happen. Train yourself and get fit! Set an intention, design a purpose, map out a path and go forward. When you have a destination, move toward it. Don't dawdle. Dawdling is idle loitering and idle loitering is a sorry waste of time. Time wasted is a lost opportunity to make money. "Go full speed ahead" as the Navy said. And I do.

Every day, I write a "to do" list. I use a Franklin Programmer right now to complete this. Create your own "to do" list and treat it as something more than a feel–good, ego-boosting directory of the amount of things you have to do. Check it off! Make it work for you. On my list, I have two columns. The first contains the things I must get done today and the second includes the things I'm thinking about that need to get done at a point in the future. Then, a bit later in the day, I chunk down the future and focus on the ASAP things, completing every one, even if I have to remain up well past my bedtime. I know that if I slack off, I'll just have to carry the list forward tomorrow and if I thought I was super busy today, I'll have a double load to face in the morning. I make a commitment to finish whatever is on my list and I try to I honor my commitment.

This listing process is a great deal more difficult than it actually sounds. There are days in which I'm totally overwhelmed and although I break my own commitment, I quickly get back on track because I realize the penalty I will have to pay the following day. Then, guilt sets in. Usually, the self-blame motivates me to turn around, head straight to my office and finish what I left undone!

It is important to recognize the consequences attached to opting for inaction. People will always strive more to shun pain than to seek pleasure. Therefore, if the consequence of not achieving an objective remains fresh in your mind, the pain it causes will motivate you to action. On the other hand, if you just consider how pleasurable it will be to slide between the sheets instead of finishing your work, you will jump into bed guilt free because there is no consequence.

I believe there comes a time in life when you realize you do something just because you do it. For me, this point arrived recently, when I hit 40. To me, 40 has a different outlook from 30. At 30, I could decide to walk, run and work out if I chose to. I would go the gym maybe a couple of times a week. If I wanted to shed a few pounds, I just wouldn't eat for a day or two and they would literally melt away. But now, at 40, I realize I bike, walk and exercise to build the bone mass needed to prevent the onset of osteoporosis in later years. I know I have to make physical activity a part of my day and I know I have to be committed or pay the penalty.

All the things that were once elective are now musts and become part of a routine, like brushing my teeth. Ten or twenty years ago, it was just a choice to take or leave, without consequence or responsibility.

I have a gentleman working for me who in the past was my personal trainer. He was 22 when he trained me last year; he worked at a 24-hour fitness center and was slender. Curiously, I watch what he eats during the day and notice his diet does not resemble that of a professional trainer. This young man eats more candy and junk food than anyone I've ever seen. Is this surprising behavior for a former fitness trainer? Not at all—he's 23 and the law of weight management has not even begun to scratch his brain.

When I asked him about his eating habits and weight gain his response was, "Tonja, I work out!" I laughed and thought to myself, "That will last so long and then all of a sudden, as he begins to age, his body will start to gain weight." If you're looking for verification, just observe the people on the planet! You will notice that very few individuals at 40 look like they did ten or twenty years previously; however, those who do have achieved their objective through serious commitment. They are accountable because they know the consequences if they let irresponsibility get the upper hand.

At 20 or 30, you act as if you're not liable for much because you have not had enough experience. As you mature, you begin to understand the value of accountability, responsibility and commitment. But more importantly, you learn that you choose to make certain commitments because of the consequences.

I call this way of reasoning "big-picture thinking" and I believe there is a specific time in life when this thought process starts to evolve. After 36, people begin to consider giving an identity to the big picture. Actually, it's the little picture of the daily activity that builds the big picture. And as you condition yourself to do certain things, the big picture begins to unfold because at this point in time, you're ready for it. You've worked conscientiously and the big picture goes, "Wow, you're prepared! Look at how disciplined you are. Look at how accountable, committed and dedicated you are concerning the choices you've made! Look at what you've done! So here is the big picture!"

Here you are, invited to look at the big picture. So, you step forward, take a look, and respond, "Huh, is this meant for me?" Then, without pausing to answer, you turn around, look behind and say, "Well of course it is. Look at all the things I've traveled through to get where I am today. Look at all the experiences I've had. Look at how I prepared myself to reach this point. I took a serious look at the design of my life plan!"

In many of my seminars, I teach a Life Binder system, which I base on my personal experiences. As a child, I tried to figure out what I wanted to do when I grew up. This figuring out process continued into my thirties. Then, one day, I got the idea to take a binder and put it together. Once assembled, I went online and downloaded my astrological chart for the entire year. I researched my auras and my chakras and created a daily schedule including affirmations, favorite quotes and sayings, as well as positive motivational testimonials. The chakras represent the body's energy field, are seven in number and are located along the spinal column.

They are converted into hormones, cells and other chemicals in the human body. The auras, on the other hand, are energy vibrations that affect the mind, emotions and spiritual component of the body.

Once I charted my energy sources, I completed the Enneagram Personality Test. This test deals with motivation and puts people in nine different categories using behavioral traits:

1. Critic—Perfectionist

2. Giver—Caretaker

3. Achiever—Succeeder

4. Romantic—Artist

5. Observer—Thinker

6. Loyalist—Devil's Advocate

7. Enthusiast—Adventurer

8. Leader—Challenger

9. Mediator—Peacemaker

My Life Binder was about studying me and my behavior patterns. I took myself on as a project and decided I was going to analyze myself and explore what made me tick, as opposed to playing "shrink" with those around me.

During the time I was married, I discovered it was far too easy for me to analyze my former husband and I guess that's the reason why he has "ex" status today. I'd examine and pick on every minute idiosyncrasy or annoying habit he had. I'd be bothered by his quirks, yet I was faultless—perfect!

One day, my ex-husband made a comment to me. "You

know, Tonja," he said, "you'd make a great psychologist!"
Actually, I was going to school and majoring in psychology at
the time.

"Tonja," he continued, "you'll have your bachelor's soon
and to get a master's, you don't need to go back to school."

"Really?" I responded, somewhat puzzled by his comment.

"No," he said. "All you have to do is study yourself—
because you have every problem you can imagine!"

He said this in such a loving way that I couldn't help but
laugh. "I think you're right," I said, "and now I know what to
do—I'll study me. After all, I'm a lot more interesting than
you!"

Well, it was just a comeback to my ex's comment. I was
serious and set out on this exploratory mission, determined
to discover what I was all about. Astrologically, I'm a Libra;
therefore, my first task was to understand the characteristics
of Librans. I had so many questions to answer: what does it
mean to be a Libra? What is the difference if you're on the
cusp? I spent time learning all about the Libra personality.
Then, I found myself questioning if it really mattered what
sign I was and if all this astrological stuff had a vein of truth
running through it. "Is it for real?" I asked myself one day.

To find the answers, I started greeting everyone I met
with the retro, "What's your sign?" line. Once I had the info,
I would read up on their sign and try to see if they fit into the
stereotype. Then, I went further and studied the Enneagram
Personality categories and applied the data to my "analysis."
I learned that there are some very distinct core character traits
in people that can be clearly identified. Once recognized, you

will be able to understand how you can interact with diverse types of individuals according to their personality makeup. This is a major step in your action plan to success. However, first and foremost, you have to be able to answer the important "Who am I?" question. And in order to find a reliable answer, you must understand yourself and all the various personality types in the world.

There are the nine Enneagram Personality Test categories, which I mentioned above. This type of character examination is more in-depth and touches on the spiritual component of the human being. Additionally, there is another personality test called the Hartman Color Code. This 45-question "driving core motive" personality assessment simplifies the results by categorizing people into four types according to color:

1. Red—Power

2. Blue—Intimacy

3. White—Peace

4. Yellow—Fun

I used both tests to analyze myself and thought, "Okay, if I'm going to be successful, I have to understand all the personality possibilities in the universe and learn how I interact with them, how they interact with me and how we react and relate to each other reciprocally. I also had to discover the traits, habits and quirks of others that disturbed me—and I had to learn why and what I could do to change this reaction pattern.

For example, I'm extremely bothered by the Yellow personality type, which is a fun loving, frivolous, pleasure-seeking individual with a zero responsibility quotient. This is the colleague or coworker who organizes and schedules all the entertainment events. Usually, they are deadline consciousness-challenged and are nonchalant about arriving on time for work. However, despite the lack of professional accountability, they are necessary because they boost morale in the office. I have to admit that it's positive to have these "class clowns" around, simply because they keep people laughing. And laughter suffocates discouragement and a host of other negative productivity slayers. Yet, despite it all, the Yellow personality type drives me nuts!

I pursued my "analytic studies" and discovered that oddly enough, in my personal relationships, I was actually attracted to these hedonistic, light-hearted individuals, whereas in business, they had me crawling the walls, frustrated and irate. Now, I questioned why and searched for an answer. My groping for answers lead me to uncover that I was a Red personality type—a disciplined, higher achiever who strives to get things done. I'm straightforward, short and cut right to the point. Therefore, in order for me to relax and have some fun, I must have a Yellow personality type in my life. Someone has to say, "Hey, Tonja, come on, let's play hooky today!"

The lesson here is that if you know and understand yourself and apply the same knowledge to people who surround you, it is easier to get along with and relate to others and more profitable to function as a team. Remember—nobody succeeds solely on their own merits.

A good example of this concept is Donald Trump's weekly *Apprentice* show. I find it fascinating to observe the group dynamics of the individuals in competition. One candidate in particular remains in my mind. Although he is an attorney, this gentleman demonstrates absolutely no social skills. His interaction with team members is beyond poor. My "diagnosis" of the situation is that as a child, someone padded and fluffed his self-esteem. Consequently, his behavior reeks of an obnoxious, "I'm better than you" pattern. He mistreats everyone miserably and best of all, he does not have a conscious awareness of his intolerable manner. His teammates, however, see the picture clearly and when they confront him, the response is an "I don't see it—it's all of you" rebuttal.

It's one thing if two people point a finger at you and forty say they don't see it, but if everyone zaps at a fault in you, it's a whole different ball game and maybe you better open your eyes to the truth. According to Lord Krishna, "The best way to help mankind is through the perfection of yourself."

Follow the principles of Johari's Window: give yourself a self-disclosure document. Be honest and list all your failings and personality traits. Then share them with those around you. Make sure you're looking at yourself through a clear windowpane, just as others do. This test will tell you what you know about yourself and what others know about you. The results will be startling, but beneficial to both your personal and professional relationships. This is one of the most valuable gifts you can give yourself.

Another exercise I have people run through in my training seminar involves listing four people they think do not like them. Try this yourself. Once you have made the selections, I advise you to approach each individual and ask them if they would sit down with you for forty-five minutes and honestly tell you all the negative things about your personality that you don't enjoy hearing. Ask them to explain how they see you and how they perceive you. Encourage them to tell you what they like and don't like about you. It will be one of the most painful and difficult things to experience, but in the end, it can turn into a beneficial exercise.

Take it to heart. Resist the urge to speak. Instead, just listen. The information they will give you will help accelerate both your personal growth and potential for wealth accumulation. It's absolutely amazing. I always advise them to pick their spouse or partner as one of the people. Do whatever it takes. Slap some Duct Tape across your mouth if you feel you can't be quiet. Because if you spend the time actually listening as opposed to disagreeing with their comments or viewing yourself in a power struggle, you can gain lightning-speed growth.

I have people run through this experiment on the first day of the workshop. Then, on the following day, I have them return to discuss the experience. It's interesting to note that the room is usually divided. Half of the people did it and felt enriched and just fabulous, while the other half admitted they couldn't get up the courage to do it. When I asked them why they backed out, they responded that it was too painful for them to even feel that someone may see them in a different way from how they perceived themselves!

I took my exercise further. I had the people who were unable to participate initially team up with those who completed the process. It was an interesting turn. They interacted, went home and did the exercises. The following day, they returned exhilarated.

One gentleman told me he could never understand why he would leave work in a great mood, come home every evening to his family, walk through the back door into the kitchen and switch into the most awful mood. As a result, he and his wife would start arguing.

"Tonja," he told me, "I've been married for 27 years and I can't count how many times I got mad when I came home."

"Well," I said, "What were you mad about?"

"You know," he replied, "I never understood what was making me angry. But during that exercise my wife told me how miserable I am. And I knew I was miserable, but I didn't know why! While she was speaking, I followed your advice. I didn't say anything. I couldn't answer her, I couldn't walk away. I just listened and thought about it. And you know what I figured out? You know why I get mad? Well, I get furious because every day for 27 years, I've walked through the back door and stepped into the kitchen. And I see a mess. It's always a disaster. My wife cooks dinner for the family and there are greasy pots and pans everywhere. I can't stand it. It looks horrendous."

"So, now that you know the reason for your mood swing," I said, "what are you going to do about it?"

"Well, Tonja, from now on, I'm going to walk in the front door!"

In 27 years, he would argue with his wife, go away and never get to the root of the problem. Nothing was ever resolved and the disturbing situation played out again and again. He never thought about isolating the reason, but kept pushing it on the back burner. This is another example of "chunking it down." The big thing was his anger, but he never bothered to discover why, or what was behind it.

My exercise allows people to get in tune with who they are

and what they need to uncover about themselves to get another perspective. The same process can be applied to the professional environment to help you discover how productive you are and how much time you really waste during the day.

Ultimately, I look at what a person generates in income and I relate it directly to a prosperity consciousness. People always debate this because it contradicts what they were taught growing up. Teachers, parents and guidance counselors always said, "Get a good education, work hard, get a career and retire after 30 years!" But nobody is taught to "Work smart!"

So, people work hard, earn a decent, manageable income but never amass great wealth. If you ask someone how much they are worth, generally, they will quote you a figure that reflects their net worth. I have to say, "No, no, I don't mean what's your net worth. I mean how much are you *worth*?"

The instinctive response is, "What do you mean?"

"Have you ever thought about what your worth is?" I ask. "Think about how much you deserve to earn every year, every singly month, every week and every day in your entire lifetime."

I have noticed that amazingly, most people do not quote a figure more than $10,000 or $20,000 above their highest salary! These people fall back on and establish their own glass ceiling, actually believing they cannot achieve the uppermost because a glass ceiling keeps them anchored at a lower level. This self-constructed expansion blockade holds them back from creating the circumstances necessary for wealth accumulation. If they are unable to shatter the glass ceiling they should, at minimum, begin to penetrate the surface by drilling some holes.

I find that people install their own glass ceilings with their consciousnesses. They say, "I made $50,000, therefore I believe that's what I'm worth! I won't be $50,001 until I believe I can make that extra dollar." Part of the action plan is actually creating the consciousness that expands your prosperity thinking. The key is to reinforce in your mind that you're worth it—that you can create the income you want. But you have to teach yourself to really want it.

This action is not as easy as it may appear. Evidence of its complexity rests in the fact that the universe is not overpopulated with multi-millionaires. Not everyone enjoys enormous wealth. When you look at a person and see their income figures, you can plainly point to where their consciousness is.

A while ago, I had a woman working for me who had been earning $17,000 a year. Previously, she had come to one of my seminars because she was interested in increasing her income. I hired her for my foundation and said, "Listen, I'll help you double your earnings. If you work evenings at the airport and have time to get seven or eight hours of sleep, you can come to the foundation at 2:00 p.m. and do some part-time work. I'll pay you the same amount you're earning at the airport. However, there is one condition: do not quit your other job, because if you leave that job, you won't be doubling your income."

She agreed, came to the foundation and five days later, she quit her airport job! Her reasoning was, "Tonja, I just didn't like it. I'm totally into this one. I totally want to be here!"

"Well, you want to be here at the expense of your future," I told her, "because your future and your financial plan were designed to keep both jobs in place for a short period of time."

Her consciousness demonstrated that even though we had the ability to double her self-worth, she took it away. We had a plan to accomplish an objective, but her thinking wouldn't allow the plan to be carried out because she nixed the principle condition when she quit her airport job. Before the plan had even a chance to work, her thoughts deleted it.

If the thinking and action are not in harmony, the objective cannot be attained. Most people feel they can think and they're done. Wrong! You have to think and do if you want achieve success. I always call it, "Treat and move your feet" because typically, in Religious Science, we do prayer treatments. We actually treat for what we envision we want in our lives. Then we take action, because it is not productive to just slouch on the couch all day and pray. You have to show your sense of commitment by getting up, taking action and moving toward your objective. If you're not willing to work smart, you won't fit into the causal millionaire mindset and you certainly will not amass great wealth! "As you sow, you shall reap!" they said in *Galatians 6:7*.

9

The "Big Win"

There is no better way to thank God for your sight than by giving a helping hand to someone in the dark.

—Helen Keller

When I first began thinking about the content I would include in the chapter titled *The Big Win*, I thought it would be a discussion regarding how I did it—how I became a multi millionaire. I started writing my own success story, but each time I read the words on the pages, I did not feel satisfied. Something was missing. I felt as if my sentences just didn't have the substance to effectively show the real process. Actually, they made it look so easy, when in fact it wasn't. This wasn't my real message!

I am so mindful about and committed to making sure

you will understand that accumulating wealth through the real estate investment process is in essence merely a process. It is neither a visionary nor flippant "get rich quick" scheme of little merit. It does, however, involve commitment and a smart work strategy.

When I was producing my *Quantum Cash* infomercial (www.tdquantumcash.com), I encountered the usual barrage of "experts," well intentioned on informing me how I should shoot it to guarantee effortless, faster and better sales figures for my product. The free advice did not end there! When I produced my TV show *Backyard Wealth,* once again people expressed ideas and perspectives regarding how the program could be made more enticing and sellable. As mentioned in an earlier chapter, I don't believe in listening to others and I'm not agreeable to following advice, thank God! Why, you might ask, am I so closed to the public voice? Well, because I find validity in the truth—somehow, it really works. And it works because it encourages people to make conscious changes using as criteria a huge dose of reality instead of meaningless chatter.

When you meet me, if your first and immediate impression is, "Tonja certainly doesn't sugar coat much of anything," I will compliment you for being an excellent character judge and personality analyst. Camouflaging or bending the truth has never been my approach, simply because I don't believe that adding a sweetener profits you in any way, manner or form. And I am certain that sugar coating the truth serves neither me nor the planet.

Instead, I believe in educating and speaking to my audience. My intention is to let them hear what nobody else is saying about real estate—the flip side, the uncoated truth, a.k.a. reality. I believe that if you have done your homework, researched your project and gathered all the correct facts, you are in an opportune position to make a conscious choice to select an option that can positively affect your financial condition, a choice that will benefit the entire family. This is why all my training programs and seminars are down to earth, basic and interactive. Each one is designed to show you how to attain your objectives. And *The Casual Millionaire* is no exception.

So, the burning question remains: how did I do it? Honestly, I just can't give you either a full description or a cut and dry answer regarding how I did it. The question seems so difficult to answer. It almost seems as if I can't remember. In all honesty, I really have to pause a moment to think! And maybe that's because at first, I did it by following my heart and my gut!

However, I will assure you that I know what it's like to be so broke that you look forward to happy hour just to get a bite to eat! On the other hand, I also know what it's like to be so wealthy that I can jet from coast to coast just for dinner.

My professional journey has taken me from flat broke to the acquisition of multi- millions in a very short period of time and has taught me how to amass great wealth from nothing. I know this works because I have lived it and I have done it. I also know that you and I share some remarkable similarities; we both have an interest in real estate and believe in being informed by keeping up with market news and trends. Well, the next step is to absorb what you read and just start doing it!

To get back to the "how"—you know that it involved working smart even if at first it was hard. And it was hard because initially, change is usually difficult until it just isn't anymore. If you really want to do it—if you're passionate about doing it—you will make the necessary decisions and take the required action to help you attain your objective. And as I discussed in an earlier chapter, you will set your intention and you will move forward!

I prepared myself by getting the right education to help me pursue my objectives. I chose real estate because I realized it was a means to achieving the wealth I wanted. It was what I liked to do. It was what I was passionate about and it was what I was good at!

Once I had acquired the knowledge I needed, I knew that to succeed, I had to put into action what I had learned—this was my "how" process. I'll share a few examples of strategies I used, but don't forget to ask the "why" question. This is the essential link to achievement because without a strong and valid reason to do it, you will neither set nor take action on an intention—that is the "why"!

In my book *Bubble Proof: Real Estate Strategies that Work in any Market,* I outlined some specific strategies on how to get started. I'm grateful that you are reading my books and would be happy if you would put the information to use so that the Big Win can be flipped to be about you instead of me.

The greatest thrill in my life is to watch you achieve your objectives and climb to success; that's what my Big Win chapter is about—you!

When I started this book and decided to title it *The*

Casual Millionaire, my strategy was to show you how to get everything you want and deserve. It is my belief that everyone deserves to have freedom of choice—the ability to choose what they want to awaken to every morning, or how they wish to present themselves, be it dressed in a business suit or shorts and a polo shirt. Although these may seem like incidentals, freedom of choice also involves financial freedom. Choose it and it's yours—this is the Big Win!

My own personal financial freedom has actually presented me with more options to choose. It's interesting to note how choosing to become financially free offers you a whole new set of choices.

Often in my seminars, I tell my audience, "Stop a minute and ask yourself what your choices would involve once you are financially free."

Perhaps you will discover that your perspectives would be different, just as the circumstances of your life. However, unless you put yourself in a position of financial freedom and walk along that path, you won't be able to answer the question. So, the next question is, how do you become financially free?

Wish it and want it! Dream it and envision it! Fake it until you get it—but make it happen! Then when you get it, learn how to say thank you and give it to someone else! I did and you can!

If you connect with the Higher Power, if you know what you want, what you like doing as well as what you're good at, and if you are willing to focus on what you're passionate about, you're on your way to accomplishing your objective. Set your intention and envision having it all—the multi-millions, the emotional security, the different choices and the ability to give back to the universe!

"I have found that among its other benefits, giving liberates the soul of the giver," said Maya Angelou, and I agree!

Then, move a step further—make a conscious choice to change! Relinquish the ideas you had to become someone or something to secure your lot in this lifetime. Be willing to accept the fact that you are already exactly who you are and begin to do what speaks to you fearlessly.

I defined, called forth and put my faith in the Higher Power Intelligence, a consciousness that I knew would support me. Then, I took full responsibility with neither restriction nor limitation. I saw my road to freedom and prosperity run through the deeper layers of accountability, liability and conscientiousness. I heightened my self-awareness, decided what I wanted to do and learned how to honestly assess my strengths and weaknesses, making use of the knowledge I had acquired to move me toward taking action on my intentions. Yes, I said intentions. Personally, I love objectives; however, I have discovered that my intentions move me beyond my objectives! I am a "doer"—I create momentum.

It isn't easy. But, you can do it if you are determined and surround yourself with people who really jazz you; people who share your enthusiasm for mental, physical and spiritual fitness; people who are willing to take the time to nurture themselves, eat properly, meditate, pray and exercise daily, setting the stage for success. Select and bond with individuals who share your passion for real estate. You will feel the company motivating and inspiring. Discipline yourself and create a balanced lifestyle and more importantly, acknowledge your blessings and learn to say thank you over and over for everything, anything and all things! Gratitude, like giving, should be an instinctive reaction to the universe.

I can show you how to make money, how to save money and how to create strategic financial plans. The one thing that I can't do for you is incite you to take ACTION. In reality, this is where the rubber meets the road. If you focus your intentions on doing, you can be a big winner. Extend your boundaries, push yourself to the utmost limits, get serious and get committed. A merger of action and education is the most powerful and profitable strategy you can employ.

In my *Jet Cash* training, which is a four–day, intensive, action-oriented training program, I actually put into action what I teach. How, you may ask, do I accomplish this? Well, I do it by taking people to a multitude of destinations to purchase properties. I jet them around on my aircraft and I encourage them to follow the two most important rules for success—simultaneous education and action! In other words, learn and practice what you learned—now!

When you meet a person who has acquired substantial wealth, you will usually see a knowledgeable, self-confident individual with strong character, an ironclad determination and untiring persistence. Successful people know they merit their wealth! I believe this is the reason why a person can win the lottery and lose the money in the blink of an eye. Deep down, they don't believe they deserve it. Ask yourself, "Why do I want it, and when will I be ready to receive it?" These seemingly simple questions require not only answers, but also a firm conviction in order for you to become financially free!

And let's not forget the passion connection. In addition, you must be willing to trust your potential and take risks.

Take some advice from Donald Trump: "Every day, you'll have opportunities to take chances and to work outside your safety net. Sure, it's a lot easier to stay in your comfort zone—in my case, business suits and real estate—but sometimes you have to take risks. When the risks pay off, that's when you reap the biggest rewards."

The choices we make have a direct effect on our lives. This is why it is of paramount importance to un-clutter our minds and clearly focus our thoughts on our intentions. When you begin to understand your deepest intention, the whole world seems to open up! It's like watching a tiny bud bloom into a beautiful flower for the first time. It begins by spreading its petals slowly, almost cautiously, then before you realize it, it blossoms. And best of all, it seems to have happened instantly—kind of like becoming the casual millionaire!

> It is one of the most beautiful compensations of life
> that no man can sincerely try to help another
> without helping himself.
>
> —Ralph Waldo Emerson

10
Success Stories

The decisions we make and the choices we implement have an astonishing effect on the success quotient we will achieve. This is one reason why it is essential to taper the focus of our thoughts and center them on our intentions. As previously discussed, it always goes back to the mindset. This is the power that fuels the achieving mechanism. Once you are able to comprehend your deepest intention, it will seem as if the universe is in tune with your thinking. Just like a bud blooms into a flower ever so slowly during its initial stage and suddenly seems to sprout almost overnight, your thoughts will gradually unwrap and then blossom, giving the impression it happened in an instant.

However, behind every success there is a process that begins with understanding the self—responding to the "Who am I?" and "What do I want?" questions! In order to arrive at the answers, I diligently pursued every means available to get to the core of my essence. To investigate my spiritual connection, I took the Enneagram Personality Test and to explore my business potential, I took the Hartman Color Code. Then, for a general confirmation of outcome, I embarked on the results-proven standard, Meyer's Briggs. Through my testing process, I scrutinized and analyzed my scores, some numerical, some color and other ENTs and ENFs. By utilizing these measuring codes, I was able to respond to the "Who am I?" Once I had this riddle solved, I was aware of my talents, capabilities and the power of my spiritual connection. Having this knowledge, I was able to proceed to the "What do I want?" part of my questioning. I knew I wanted millions and I knew I could and would achieve my objective if I set my intention and concentrated on doing whatever it would take to get it materialized. Then, once I succeeded, to complete the cycle, I set another intention: to help others attain the object of their intention.

I will share an experience I had with two highly intelligent, well-educated, African American brothers. One of the gentlemen, Joe, was a conservative whose only asset was his home. Joe decided to enroll in one of my training seminars and upon completion, ended up purchasing two triplexes. He accumulated a $200,000 profit after selling one and became a partner in ten other properties, holding one eighth of an ownership share. And it didn't end there—"Mr. Conservative" then invested in a condo conversion. In addition, the value of his house skyrocketed!

Initially, Joe enrolled in my training program about three years ago because he had a son born with several physical

challenges, which required an expensive therapy regime.
Shortly thereafter, he had a healthy second son, followed by
a third. Now, he was the father of three boys and his objective was to be able to provide for his family. Joe knew he had
to make a decision to step out of his conservative box if he
wanted to achieve his intention. He had to get involved in
something that would generate a sizeable income to meet his
growing family's needs.

To satisfy the phenomenal cost arising from his first son's
medical issues, Joe was eventually forced to consider selling
one of his triplexes. Although the fees were initially covered
by his insurance carrier, eventually he received a communication informing him they felt they had overpaid. Joe's financial responsibility was evaluated at over $100,000. He was
devastated and sought a way to alleviate the debt without
having to walk away from it.

One day, he approached me. "Tonja," he said, explaining
his dilemma. "I have little choice but to sell one of the properties. I have to take care of my son's medical bills. Can you
give me a hand?"

The triplex was sold and it rescued him from serious
financial debt while providing him with enough funds to
obtain coverage for his son. Had he not made the decision
three years ago to attend my training seminar and learn about
real estate investment strategies, he would not have been in a
position today to take care of his family's special needs.

Although this may not be a multi-million dollar success
story, it is about the accomplishment of one man's objective.
Joe is an average guy trying to take care of his responsibilities
as a husband and father. He set an intention to boost his

income in order to fulfill his obligations, explored and discovered the means to attainment and moved forward by enrolling in my training seminar. Joe had all the ingredients for success and the power of his intention led him to follow the right path to his destination. He had set in place a fruitful, income-generating strategy with his investments.

About a year ago, I received a phone call from Joe. "Tonja," he said, "I was wondering if you would take some time to talk to my brother?"

"Okay, Joe," I responded. "What's happening with your brother?"

"Well, Tonja," he explained, "Jeff got involved in real estate and bought about seven properties out in Ohio. The point is, he thinks he got taken during the purchase because today, they are not worth anything."

"Joe," I said, "what do you mean they're not worth anything?"

"He bought them with 100 percent financing," Joe continued. "And although I don't know every detail, I know he believes he got taken!"

I called Jeff and listened to his story. He told me he had met the owners, who assured him he could create great cash flow by investing in the properties. Apparently satisfied with what he heard, he purchased seven properties that contained about eleven units.

Soon after, a fire broke out, causing one of the properties to burn down to the ground. The insurance company reimbursed the loss but the problem was that Jeff did not have wide enough coverage. As a result, he was thrown upside down. The irony of the situation was that Jeff worked for an insurance company, yet was negligent about obtaining suitable indemnity for his own property.

"Jeff," I said, after listening to the sequence of events. "Have you ever owned any property before you got involved in this deal?"

"No, Tonja, just my home. Can you help me out of this mess?" he responded.

"Okay," I said. "I'll fly out to Ohio and take a look."

Jeff hired me on the spot as his consultant. I flew out to Ohio, previewed his properties and returned. I discovered that he had one of the seven properties in escrow. The Realtor had it listed with a sales price of $64,000, although the market value exceeded $100,000! I phoned Jeff and said, "Why are you selling the property for $64,000?"

"Tonja," he responded, "the agent told me that's all I can get for it!"

"Jeff," I said, "if I were you, I would immediately cancel the escrow. The property is worth about $115,000! To give it away for $64,000 is crazy!"

I also discovered that he arranged for the property manager to leave keys in all the mailboxes, which made it feasible for me to get inside and look around. When I arrived and reached in to grab a key, I found they were missing! I called Jeff and said, "Listen, I'm here at the property and can't get in because there are no keys in the mailboxes! Jeff, I don't trust your property manager! Who is the agent who is listing the place?"

"My property manager," he responded.

I repeated, "Jeff, I don't trust your property manager. I just don't have a good feeling about this arrangement."

Even though I did not have the keys, I was determined to preview Jeff's properties. I knocked on the doors of the inhabited units and literally talked my way in. The tenants were accommodating and allowed me access into their homes. I took a long good look and called Jeff. Before I could address the issue he blurted, "Tonja, I think I'm going to let the properties go into foreclosure!"

"Jeff," I said, "you would be crazy to do that! If you go into foreclosure you will lose all the money you invested to maintain the properties for the past two years!"

"Well, Tonja," he said, sighing, "I just can't afford to continue doing this!"

After speaking with him for a while, I discovered he had equity in his home, a home equity line of credit, his mortgage payment on the properties did not excecd $3,000 a month and four of the seven were occupied by tenants producing a monthly income of $2,000. His negative was $1,000 and only because he failed to have the properties suitably repaired to attract a tenant.

My investigating lead me to uncover that the property manager, instead of renewing his tenants' terminated leases, was actually moving them to other units not owned by Jeff. When questioned about this tenant-stealing phenomenon, he told Jeff, "They just packed up and left!" I received the confirmation that my gut feeling was correct—Jeff's property manger was irresponsible and not trustworthy!

The amazing factor in this story was that Jeff had purchased the properties sight unseen, which is not a very wise business strategy. If you're investing that kind of money, it is essential to physically visit the property before putting an offer on it.

I asked Jeff when he had last visited the properties and his response was, "I saw them about six months ago!" When I investigated further, asking when he had first previewed them, I discovered that visit marked his first and last physical contact with the properties.

"Jeff," I said, "didn't you go take a look at the closing?"

"No," he said. "I trusted the agent!"

"Well, Jeff," I responded, "that was your first mistake!"

I set up a meeting with him to review all the documentation. He was relentless in insisting he got taken in the deal because, as he put it, "I saw that a $25,000 check was cut to the person who sold me the property." In reality, someone did an assignment on the deal, which fell within legal boundaries, and received the $25,000 as payment. I explained it to him.

Jeff was reluctant to borrow from his home equity line to pay for the properties and preferred to go into foreclosure. He was on the verge of filing for bankruptcy when I said, "Listen, Jeff, do you realize that if you file a bankruptcy, any money that is not homestead protected on your property is subject to the bankruptcy?"

He was totally unaware of the consequences he faced if he decided in favor of the foreclosure option. Jeff was desperate and would have done anything, had I not intervened, to avoid having to pay for his properties. He failed to realize what a tremendous loss he would incur utilizing the strategy he was leaning towards.

After I explained to him what he was really facing and the

penalty he would suffer, I said, "Okay, Jeff, why don't we do this: it sounds like what you don't want to do is pay for these properties on your own. So why don't you put them into a partnership? We'll get a couple of people together who are agreeable to contribute financially to this project and willing to go out and manage the properties."

He agreed with my suggestion and we put together a partnership of four, which included his brother, Joe, myself and one other person I personally brought in. At this point, he had four people involved. As a result of the partnership, Jeff was in a good position to help accumulate the $150,000 needed to rehab the properties. Once rehabbed, the units would be brought up to top market value and rented. Now, the properties were projected to cash flow about $3,000 a month!

Following my advice, Jeff avoided bankruptcy and did not have to go into foreclosure because I was able to find an alternate strategy to help him keep his assets intact as opposed to forfeiting everything, including his credit rating.

The interesting point to consider with the "brothers parable" is that one brother had been taking real estate investing courses with me for almost three years, whereas the other operated on his own without consulting anyone. Hardheaded and inflexible, he refused to seek advice and moved forward with a "Just do it" mind set! Often, I would tell him, "Jeff, stop talking and listen a moment!"

Finally, I was able to get through his hard head! The "prodigal" brother actually paid attention to what I or Joe said and made the decision to save the transaction, instead of foolishly getting rid of all his properties.

I remember when Joe came to me and said, "Tonja, I know Jeff doesn't have to go into foreclosure, but he just refuses to listen to me!" In the end, he came to his senses, recognizing he lacked training and knowledge, and allowed Joe and I to handle the situation from a different perspective.

The value of this story is that it demonstrates the power information has in attaining the Big Win! The brother who took the time to enroll in my real estate training programs was better equipped to invest profitably. In addition, he had a smoother time distinguishing between a good deal and a less likely to render or "lemon" transaction. His path to the accumulation of wealth was more consistent with success and certainly easier to follow, thus leading him directly to his objective. The other brother finally arrived, but because he failed to educate himself, he had to struggle through a thorny journey and risked the "big loss" before he enjoyed success.

In my seminars, training programs and books, I continually reinforce the value and importance of information. As discussed in this book, information involves finding the answers to the questions that will determine your outcome in any endeavor you undertake. I educate, motivate and encourage the people who come to me for advice and training, and I invite and help them discover the key to personal and professional success, which is hidden in, "Who am I? What do I want? What do I like to do? How can I do what I like to do and earn millions?" Giving a little to acquire knowledge often brings a fruitful harvest.

I had originally planned to conclude *The Casual Millionaire* by discussing the success stories of Joe and Jeff, two brothers with different approaches to business. However, when I was midway through the chapter, I remembered the many students who had not quite achieved their objectives and I thought that talking about their journeys would be beneficial as a learning tool and perhaps easier for everyone to relate to.

I believe the key to success is the ability to identify the things which keep you from achieving what you say you REALLY want. In addition, it involves setting in motion the intention to make the decision to do something to change both that faulty pattern and the flawed beliefs that stop you!

It is important to understand that often during your journey to reach a different destination, you will be involved in a process that may feel wrong and consequently uncomfortable. At this point, you can begin to feel afraid or intimidated. When fear appears and you are not conditioned to deal with it, you will react to it as you always have, with the fight or flight response! You have just two options—either you fight by resisting the thought, idea or concept or else you go into flight mode. You find yourself running away, escaping from the scene to avoid the uneasiness.

This is why it is essential to learn how to deal with the circumstances and situations that make you fearful or anxious. Are you terrified by the thought that you don't have enough money? If you answered yes, ask yourself why! More than likely, your fear will be linked to some past experience, and if you take the time to explore it, you will discover it is based on some event or occurrence that happened years ago. Our most dominant fears and uncertainties will always be manifested either consciously or otherwise, until or unless we take a proactive approach and work on uncovering the reasons behind these anxious feelings and altering the beliefs that misguide our successes.

I will share with you one of my most difficult experiences as a mentor. They involve teaching people strategies we all know will work for them, beyond a shadow of a doubt, and then having to stand by and watch as they just give up! Some people get so close to attaining success and then they do something ridiculous to sabotage it. Once the self-disrupt tactic comes into full play, they begin to look for excuses to make themselves feel better about letting go and giving up. Unfortunately, they look towards the people who were actually, really helping them and begin to cast blame in that direction! I think the finger pointing process allows them to justify their actions and gets them off the hook regarding any decision they may have made, especially if others "told them so" previously!

I've had people who I helped earn hundreds of thousands of dollars make bad decisions in an instant—choices that turned all their hard work into failure, taking their profit with it. To rationalize the poor result, they blamed me, claiming I showed them a bad deal. In reality, you could just sit back and see the deal was designed for success. It was so obvious, yet they failed because they simply didn't do what they knew they should have done in order to achieve their objective. I believe that if you refuse to take responsibility for the investments you make, most likely, you should not be investing!

Let me tell you a few stories about some could have been, "if only" successes!

Arthur's story is one of my favorites. This gentleman had

two triplexes under contract for $500,000 each. As a non-owner occupied purchase, Arthur obtained 100 percent financing on each unit, which I'll admit isn't the easiest loan to put together. His transaction had gone from a sixty-day escrow into multiple extensions that eventually put the escrow at nearly seven months.

One day Arthur came to my office. "Tonja," he said, "I've been thinking about the triplexes and I want to cancel the escrow."

"Are you sure?" I asked. "We're ready to close. The lender will issue docs in another week."

"I'm sure!" he said. "It's not meant to be, and besides, I feel like I'm wasting time waiting for this to close, whereas I could be doing something else to make money."

Okay, let's analyze this situation. Arthur has 100 percent financing. The agents, the brokers and the seller are doing all the work—therefore, wasn't it possible for him to "do other things," anyway? Why did he feel he had to wait idly? Now, get this: "Arthur," I told him, "I'm very sure that according to market value, each of those properties is worth at least $539,000! So, at closing, you've already earned $39,000 per property with one hundred percent financing!"

Unfortunately, Arthur just couldn't see it because he was stuck on the fact that the deal took too long! Side note: what he failed to realize was that *time* made him the money. So, he cancelled out and walked away!

The next day, we had a new buyer for the triplexes and new appraisals were ordered. Well, the figure came in at $539,000! Paul, the new buyer, had the same deal as Arthur regarding the 100 percent financing. His escrow took five months. When the properties closed, they were worth $560,000. Paul's escrow was not without difficulty. He encountered many challenges, from credit issues to documentation requirements regarding insurance, in addition to some last minute, irritating issues. However, unlike Arthur, he was persistent, did what he needed to do and closed. This is a success story because this was Paul's fourth property and he didn't have to make a mortgage payment while it was appreciating because it was still in escrow. Arthur could have had that same deal had he not been so anxious to "do something else!" Having personal follow-up knowledge of both men's business doings, I can tell you that Arthur did not do anything else with his time except forfeit a potential profit.

Another story centers on Eric, a very smart corporate America guy earning a rather attractive, rather hefty salary. This gentleman purchased a four unit building that had all the paperwork nearly completed for a condo conversion. He bought the property for $550,000. Each unit was under contract to sell at $255,000. However, Eric procrastinated. He failed to complete the paperwork with the city, never finalized the conversion and still holds the four unit building! If you ask Eric what happened, you'll get a monotone chorus of hemming and hawing, "Gee I don't knows," plus lots of invalid reasons why! The bottom line: Eric's lack of follow-up or follow through caused him to lose a lucrative deal!

Next in line is Terrie, a school nurse who bought a sixteen unit building for $654,000. Terrie has very little knowledge of real estate and investing and doesn't have Eric's business aptitude. She is, however, a tenacious woman with a belief in the follow-up and follow through strategy in whatever she does. Terrie got involved in a condo conversion and put together partners to help her finance the cost of the conversion. The projected conversion time was approximated at six months to a year. What no one factored into the equation was the hurricane that hit Florida. The after-effect put a slow down on the project and three years later, the conversion was not yet completed. Some of the investors became anxious and started saying, "Terrie, this isn't what we were told it would be. Never mind the hurricane—we want to take our money, put it where it can earn money and do something else with it."

Terrie accommodated them and refunded their investment. She got the building appraised and received a construction loan for $2,000,000. She used the funds to pay off the initial debt and reimburse the money she had initially invested to carry the property. In the end, she had enough funds to complete the conversion. Each unit is projected to close at $300,000—I'll let you do the math! Perhaps the people who pulled out of the deal had their reasons, but Terrie certainly will have the profit!

A postscript to Terrie: she pre-sold four units at $69,000 each to Melinda, who eventually bailed before the closing. Was she in too much of a hurry? No—she just couldn't wait and wanted to buy something. I don't know if she did, but I do know this: had Melinda bought the four condos, she'd have nearly a million dollars! Do you see the pattern so far?

The people who pulled out were governed by an instant gratification mechanism! They couldn't conceive of anything to do with their money other than spend it—and I bet most of them did!

I've watched people put together partnerships to own 10, 15, 20 and 30 properties and then complain they have to pay a $200 per month negative. It's all a question of perception— I see those negatives both as investments and tax deductions. Investing is perception; it's all about how you look at it!

I've watched people willing to pay $150,000 in fees just to refinance a property to eliminate the same $200 per month expenditure. If they were clever investors, they would have come up with the monthly $200. However, they didn't want to because they weren't actively involved in their investment and therefore didn't see the reason to let go of the money! Instead, they gave away their equity! Many times, I strongly advised people against that decision, but they went ahead and did it anyway.

I've seen people continue to pay negatives on properties which were only vacant because they needed some rehab work in order to entice a tenant to sign a lease. If you invest a little money to renovate or repair a property, you can override your negative cash flow and earn by renting it. If you maintain it *status quo*, you can only expect to keep paying a negative. Real estate is basic common sense, but common sense seems to have diverse meanings to different people.

From my training seminars and business experiences, I have gathered numerous success stories. If you look around, you will spot them everywhere. They are among your friends and relatives, in your neighborhood, in the media, in your country and around the world. They are linked to neither race, creed, social status nor professional category. However empowering they may be, the sad truth remains—there could be so many more. And there could be yours!

I want you to create your own success story! I want you to become acquainted with the reality of investing. It is neither easy nor effortless, and anyone who tells you the contrary is either not being honest or not doing it successfully! Investing is fun, energizing, challenging, rewarding, frustrating, confusing, scary, lucrative and much, much more. But, easy it's not. Investing requires discipline, education, training, commitment, a connection to yourself and your intentions, accountability, diligent work and taking responsibility.

If you use the stories I've included in *The Casual Millionaire* to help you gain knowledge and perspective, you will be surprised to see how investing can be made easier, even if never easy!

I've probably said this a zillion times to my students, the people who frequent my seminars, my friends and business colleagues, and to everyone and anyone who seeks my advice. Still, people fall and will continue to fall for the "get rich quick while you sleep" approach. Hmmm…how else can I say it, so *you* will do it differently? Or, maybe after reading *The Causal Millionaire,* you will be convinced that what I'm telling you—and, more importantly, what I am giving you— is basically the key to success, a chance to accumulate great wealth and have fun while doing it!

Tonja Demoff

About Tonja

Tonja Demoff is an entrepreneur who has invested her life in traditional and non-traditional forms of education. She believes strongly in any form of education that creates the results a person most desires in their own life. Tonja is always at the top of the game! Whatever the challenge, whatever the goal she masters it! Tonja knows how to succeed, how to be a winner, how to lead, how to focus and she knows how to make money! Her passion is in helping people get what they desire! She believes that at minimum everyone can be a millionaire just by doing a few things in a new way!

Special Events

Tonja desires for everyone to get involved and achieve a new level of personal fulfillment. Give yourself the tools to take immediate action in your life by attending one of Tonja's live events. Experience for yourself the energy and strategies required for becoming responsible for your personal growth at one of these incredible life-changing training events.

Books

In addition to *The Casual Millionaire*, Tonja has also authored *Bubble Proof – Real Estate Strategies That Work In Any Market*. With uncanny insight and old-fashioned determination, Tonja has soared from a flat-broke visionary to the top of her own business empire. How? By investing wisely in single-family homes and multi-units that doubled, tripled, even quadrupled her money. Tonja also shows why the housing market is poised to rise for years, taking smart investors along on the ride to even greater profit and financial security.

www.tonjademoffcompanies.com   *More Info On Next Page*

Tonja Demoff

Speaking Engagments

Tonja Demoff has traveled around the world to teach others how to enhance their lives and increase their income. She has inspired tens of thousands of people to take action, to experience results, and to live up to their true potential. Tonja knows people and she understands how to "turn them on" helping them move forward creating an energy that moves them at mega speed step by step! To book Tonja as a guest speaker please use the following contact information.

Contact Tonja Demoff
For any and all questions please send Tonja an email at:
tonja@tonjademoffcompanies.com

Products

Tonja has discovered the most valuable form of education, experience! This is why her teachings are so incredibly experiential. "She's just real… what you see is what you get!" Tonja has packaged her knowledge and experience into some form of media so that you can achieve the results you desire most out of your life. Tonja teaches you everything from how to buy your first home to investing with partners as well as what it takes to succeed in life, both mentally and financially.

The following is a list of available products:

*Believe and Achieve
*The Real Estate Millionaire Mindset
*Credit Repair Secrets
*First-Time Home Buyers Boot Camp
*Quantum Cash
*Partnering For Profits
*Financial Freedom Seminar System

Please visit www.tonjademoffcompanies.com to learn more about Tonja Demoff and how you can attend one of her incredible events as well as purchase additional books and products.

About the Authors

Alix and Ronald Gavran are personal growth facilitators. Their dream relationship brought forth and clearly defined their life's work—helping others to grow into a process of helping themselves. They offer workshops and other programs to assist you on the journey to Your Dream Relationship.

If you would like to be notified of a workshop or other program with Alix and Ronald, or if you would like to sponsor or organize such a workshop or program in your area, please contact them by writing to:

Alix ∞ Ronald Gavran
P.O. Box 22272
Santa Fe, NM 87502
USA